Politics of the Nineteen Twenties

Politics of the Nineteen Twenties

EDITED BY J O H N L. S H O V E R
University of Pennsylvania

GINN–BLAISDELL

A Xerox Company

WALTHAM, MASSACHUSETTS / TORONTO / LONDON

Primary Sources in American History

CONSULTING EDITOR

Grady McWhiney, University of British Columbia

99121

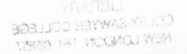

Foreword

Thorough understanding of the events and trends that make up our history cannot be acquired merely by reading textbook interpretations. It is essential also to study the basis of such interpretations. *The Primary Sources in American History Series* provides the student with materials in the form of letters, diaries, memoirs, pamphlets, and newspaper accounts written during or shortly after major historical events — documents up to now buried in the library and often unavailable.

Edited and introduced by a leading scholar, each volume either concentrates on discussion of a given topic in contemporary letters, newspaper articles, and essays or presents new editions of classic eyewitness accounts of significant events. Though generations removed from an actual occurrence, the student has the opportunity to understand it in depth and to apply his analytical and critical powers to it. He then also can compare his own interpretations with those provided by general histories, biographies, and monographs.

GRADY MCWHINEY

Contents

Introduction

Party politics between 1920 and 1930 was a sterile wasteland —
a dull preface to the more dramatic depression politics of the
following decade. Progressivism was dead. The triumphant
Republican conservatives, victors in three landslide presidential
elections, put into effect a policy of "normalcy" that returned
the country to limited government, and the pro-business policies
of the Cleveland-McKinley era.

These common generalizations about politics in the twenties
are not categorically wrong, but they are exaggerated and over-
simplified. Representatives and Senators of Progressive inclina-
tion constituted the principal opposition to the policies of
Republican presidents and cabinets. They harassed successive
administrations through Congressional investigations, blocked
and modified key administration programs, and struggled to
realize alternative policies in such important areas as farm
relief and public power. Moreover, the impressive electoral
victories of Harding, Coolidge, and Hoover obscure the fact
that Republican control of Congress was never commensurate
with the Presidential victory margins. The party's margins of
control in Congress slipped in each non-presidential election;
a sizable minority of Republican Congressmen openly rebelled
against the policies proclaimed by their own party's administrative leaders.

The twenties was a period of transition for both major political parties. A pattern of Republican dominance in presidential politics, shaped in the 1890s and broken only by the two inconclusive Wilson victories (one against the divided Republicans in 1912, the other the paper thin margin of 1916) was slowly being eroded. Throughout the decade, the sectional coalition of rural and mountain West with the solid South that had dominated the Democratic party since the silver battles of 1894 and 1896 was increasingly challenged by powerful Democratic machines in the nation's major cities.

The instability of both the Republican and Democratic party in the twenties can be understood more readily if the American party system is conceived as encompassing four parties, not two. As James MacGregor Burns has suggested, these are: the presidential Republicans, the Congressional Republicans, the presidential Democrats, and the Congressional Democrats. Not only is the President elected for a different term than Senators or Representatives, but the latter two, due to their geographically circumscribed constituency, are more acutely responsive to local pressures while presidential candidates must coalesce sectional appeals and speak in more general terms of overall national policy.

Within the Democratic party the rising urban tide was far more evident in the battles for the nomination of presidential candidates than in the Southern-dominated party Congressional delegation. For example, Governor Alfred E. Smith of New York, candidate in 1928 of the northern, urban wing of the party, failed to carry areas of the South where Democratic Congressmen were elected virtually without opposition.

In the dominant Republican party, voters who cast their ballots for Harding, Coolidge, or Hoover often showed a perverse tendency to vote for either Democratic Congressional candidates or for Republican insurgents who opposed nearly every administration program. Inside the Congress, given the narrow margin of Republican control, small groups of dissidents, largely Republicans, who were organized variously as the farm or Progressive bloc, often held the balance of power. Throughout the decade they allied with Democrats occasionally to thwart and often to frustrate policies advanced by the Presidential Republicans. Often they took the initiative to advance legislation that ran counter to the policies and programs of their party's titular leaders. Thus, Secretary of Treasury Andrew Mellon's tax reduction plan of 1921 was not fully implemented by Congress until 1926; the McNary-Haugen plan for farm relief, a proposal alien to the agricultural policies of the Republican administrations, twice passed both houses of a Republican dominated Congress and was twice vetoed by President Coolidge. A veteran's bonus was passed over the veto of Coolidge. Late in the decade Congress approved public ownership of the power facilities at Muscle Shoals, Alabama and, predictably, President Hoover vetoed the legislation. Passage of such important administration legislation as the Fordney-McCumber Tariff of 1921 and the Immigration Act of 1924 was possible only because most Republican Progressives supported them. In fact, the major opposition to the policies of the Republican administrations in the twenties came not from the conservative and schism-torn Democrats but from dissident Republicans in Congress.

Politics, however, involves issues as well as processes. What was the output of the political process of the twenties in terms of decisions made and policies clearly articulated? Due to the stalemate within the parties, the record of accomplishment was meager. The decade was more significant for issues posed and evaded than for issues confronted. Only one Congressional enactment, the Immigration Act of 1924, can be said to have had long term consequences. Of the questions that provoked the major political controversies of the twenties, only a few attempted to formulate political responses to new circumstances created by the accelerating social and economic changes taking place in the decade. Most of the political debate centered on attempts to cope with decisions that had been made in the past. Prohibition hung like a pall over politics — more than any other single issue it splintered and immobilized the Democratic party.

Problems of railway transportation, the question of disposition of the government-built merchant marine, the Mellon tax program, all sprang from decisions made during the war years.

The selections that follow attempt to interlace processes and issues as they are in the real political world. The words and thoughts are those of contemporary observers and they range from the articulate and penetrating observations of Walter Lippmann to the myopic, naive excuses of Charles Forbes, a guilt-laden malfeasant in one of the grossest scandals of the Harding administration.

The five chapters that follow are arranged more or less in chronological order. The first, focusing on electoral behavior in the Harding years, reveals the extent to which observers, both journalistic and academic, regarded their own political era as one of instability, not stability. The second attempts to re-create some of the issues of the presidential contest of 1924 and raises such questions as why the Harding scandals had so little political effect, why La Follette in defeat was the most successful third party candidate since Theodore Roosevelt and why the Democratic party collapsed so completely. Chapter Three breaks from the chronological sequence and is concerned with four of the critical political questions debated in the decade. It views these in the context of the persistent battle waged between Congress and the executive branch throughout the decade. Chapter Four examines briefly the lackluster campaign and elections of 1926, one journalist observing it in the narrow perspective of the time and Walter Lippmann generalizing from the indecisive results to an explanation of the political indifference that to him characterized the twenties. The final chapter samples some of the divergent opinion that made the election of 1928 one of the most bitter in American political history and concludes with a careful contemporary attempt to explain the results.

For those participants whose words appear here, the politics of their era was neither sterile nor meaningless. Progressivism was not dead nor was normalcy the inviolate order of the day.

Perhaps among these commentaries the reader may find, as the editor has, some suggestive comparisons with another era of political change and ambivalence — the one in which we live.

JOHN L. SHOVER

PARTY VOTE FOR PRESIDENT, 1920–1928

Year	Republican	%	Democratic	%	Progressive	%	Other	%
1920	16,153,115	60.3	9,133,092	34.1			1,482,406	5.6*
1924	15,719,921	54.0	8,386,704	28.8	4,826,471	16.5	161,927	.7
1928	21,437,277	58.2	15,007,698	40.8			360,976	1.0

PARTY STRENGTH IN CONGRESS, 1921–1931

		SENATE			HOUSE		
Year	Congress	R	D	Other	R	D	Other
1921–23	67th	59	37		300	132	1
1923–25	68th	51	43	2	225	207	3
1925–27	69th	54	40	1	247	183	5
1927–29	70th	48	47	1	237	195	3
1929–31	71st	56	39	1	267	163	1
1931–33	72nd	48	47	1	218	216	1†

* Eugene V. Debs, Socialist, polled 919,799 (3.4%) in 1920.
† The Senate had 96 members, the House, 435. Democrats organized the House in 1931 due to Republican vacancies.

CHAPTER 1

The Changing American Electorate: The Harding Years

Warren G. Harding in 1920 won the greatest percentage of the two party vote of any presidential candidate in history. The Republican party, solidly united for the first time since 1908, swept into decisive control of both houses of Congress. The post-election editorial in *Current Opinion*, which follows, describes the dimensions of the Republican landslide and interprets it less as a partisan victory than as evidence that the American electorate was volatile and party allegiances were rapidly changing.

A brief two years later, the voters lent credence to *Current Opinion*'s analysis. The pendulum swung nearly as sharply in the opposite direction and, in what the liberal *Nation* termed "Election by Disgust Again," the Republicans lost 8 seats in the Senate and 75 in the House. Stuart A. Rice, Professor of Government at Dartmouth College, a pioneer in the behavioral study of politics, concluded on the basis of these results that traditional party alignments were disintegrating and new ones being formed. Professor Rice did not postulate what form these would take, but his careful appraisal of alternative political coalitions serves as a useful basemark for evaluating party development through the course of the decade.

The issue of prohibition enforcement, according to Rice, was a major factor in the puzzling political fluctuations of the twenties. Governorships and Congressional seats often hinged more upon a candidate's stand, wet or dry, than upon his party affiliation. In a number of states (for example, California, New York, Illinois), bitter political contests were provoked by attempts to repeal the "Little Volstead Acts" that provided for supplementary state enforcement of the 18th amendment. In several states the repeal efforts were successful. Prohibition lent substance to the rural-urban schism in the Democratic party and was a major cause of the party's ineffectiveness. From the many discussions of this question, a *Literary Digest* preview in 1922 of the forthcoming Congressional and state elections has been selected as illustrating the significance of the prohibition issue.

The Landslide and Its Meanings, *Current Opinion, LXIX, December 1920, pp. 757–61*

Nothing like it, for size, has ever before been seen in our political history. Eight years ago the Republican party had but eight votes in the Electoral College and less than three and one-half million votes in the ballot boxes. Last month, according to the latest figures available at this writing, it will have 404 electoral votes (out of a total of 531) and its popular *plurality* is considerably over six million votes. Not one state above the old Mason and Dixon's line is left in the Democratic column, and not all of those below. Three of the border states — Delaware, Maryland and Missouri — went Republican, the latter by about 120,000 — and the fourth, Kentucky, while giving a small plurality to Cox, seems to have elected Ernst, Rep., to the U. S. Senate by a larger plurality than Cox received. More than this, Tennessee, for the first time, gives a plurality to the Republican candidate for President, and New Mexico and Oklahoma do likewise. In the northern states such unprecedented pluralities — due in large part, of course, to the large increase in the number of voters, owing to woman suffrage — are recorded as over

1,000,000 in New York, 720,000 in Pennsylvania, 800,000 in Illinois, and about 400,000 each in Ohio, Massachusetts, Michigan and Iowa. In New York City Harding received a plurality of 440,000, every boro falling into line behind him. But even these figures fail to indicate the full dimensions of the landslide. The Republican majority in the House of Representatives seems to have reached the unprecedented total of 179, the figures being 307 Republicans, 127 Democrats, 1 Socialist. Missouri will send but 2 Democrats to the next Congress (out of 16). There will not be a Democratic congressman from any of the following states, namely: Connecticut, Delaware, Idaho, Illinois, Indiana, Iowa, Kansas, Maine, Michigan, Minnesota, Montana, Nevada, New Mexico, North Dakota, Ohio, Oregon, Rhode Island, South Dakota, Utah, Vermont, Washington, West Virginia, Wisconsin, Wyoming — 24 states in all — unless the final official canvass discloses errors in the count. . . .

The Senate shows the effects of the landslide less than the House because only 34 Senators were elected this year. Out of these, the Republicans elected 25, capturing 10 from the Democrats and losing none. This gives them a majority in the next Senate of 22, the figures standing 37 Democrats, 59 Republicans. . . .

Such are the outlines of the most tremendous sweep ever made by a political party in America. More complete details will be needed to disclose to what extent the result was affected by the votes of the women. In Tennessee, for instance, reports tell of a "tremendous" vote by the women in the mountain districts, adding greatly to the Republican vote. But the very size of the result makes it impossible to put one's finger on this or that particular factor as the cause. The best that can be done is to say that while Harding and Coolidge were elected, the victory was won by General Grouch. This seems to be the general view. The *Nation* calls it an "election by disgust." The N. Y. *Herald* remarks that political avalanches such as this do not spring from the personal popularity of candidates but are "the expression of an embittered people," its inference being, of

course, that "Wilsonism" is the cause of the embitterment. The
N. Y. *Times* thinks that the embitterment comes from deep-
seated economic troubles and the childlike faith of the American people that such troubles can be remedied by politics and
politicians. Ever since the armistice, it says, Republican politicians have been encouraging that faith and manufacturing discontent. Mr. Harding will now have to face the stern realities
of a situation in which the prosperity of the country is inextricably involved in conditions pertaining to all countries and
which are not to be remedied by the formula "America first."
The Nebraska *State Journal* finds the result due "to popular
discontents with inconveniences suffered under the Democratic
administration," and finds such solace as may be found in the
belief that "the Republicans are going in at a time to assume
the odium for an unprosperous period." The N. Y. *Evening
Post* sees in the vote for Harding "a mighty wave of protest"
and analyzes it as follows:

> We are in the backwash from the mighty spiritual and phys-
> ical effort to which America girded herself when she won the
> war for the Allies and saved the world from a fate which Amer-
> ica would again challenge if the need arose. The war has not
> been repudiated, tho the Administration that fought it has been
> overwhelmed. We are now in the chill that comes with the
> doctor's bills. As we see it now, any man in the Presidency, and
> any party in power, would have met the same punishment that
> was meted out yesterday to Woodrow Wilson. and the Demo-
> cratic party. Any Administration that conducted the war would
> now be the target of the bewildering number of protests that
> merged yesterday into one gigantic protest.

One other deduction may safely be drawn and is generally
accepted. No such overwhelming result can be taken as a partizan victory. In fact, taken with preceding elections, the conclusion is inevitable that the recent election is a proof not of
growing partizan strength but of growing partizan weakness.
It means that a very large part of the voting population is ready
to swing easily from one party to another, unhampered by traditions. Eight years ago the Democrats held a majority of 163

votes in the House of Representatives and the early death of the Republican party, with its eight electoral votes, was freely predicted. Millions of voters, disgruntled with the Taft administration, swung lightly out of the party then and have swung as lightly back again now. The city of New York furnishes a startling revelation. On the same day that it gave 440,000 plurality to Harding it gave about 325,000 plurality to Al Smith, Democratic candidate for Governor. Political observers, so the Philadelphia *North American* remarks, know that so violent a swing of the pendulum as took place last month will inevitably be followed by a reverse movement. They read in the staggering figures of the vote "no outburst of enthusiastic partizanship but rather the opposite — evidence of a spirit of independence and insurgency." Referring to the diverse elements rallying to Harding's support, the Omaha *World-Herald* says of the Republican campaign: "It cemented together 'Wall Street' power and Non-partizan League votes. It wrapped radicals and reactionaries in close embrace. It appealed alike to anti-league Republicans, pro-league Republicans and anti-league Democrats — even to some pro-league Democrats. It put Bryan to bed with Penrose and cavalier with covenanter, bestowing its benignant blessing on all alike. It promised all things to all men — and today it awakens to its morning of solemn responsibility."

Election by Disgust Again, *The Nation, 115, November 22, 1922, p. 540*

Just as was the case two years ago it was an election by disgust. Once more the electorate turned the rascals out, but never before in our political history has there been so startling and so wide-spread a reversal of an overwhelming verdict rendered only two years before. No one would have ventured to suggest then that within twenty-four months New Hampshire, Oregon, Washington, and Kansas would be carried by the Democrats, and a Democratic Governor elected in New York by a plurality of more than 400,000. The pendulum has swung back almost as far as it could have. The question remains, however, what has really been accomplished, and whether we have done anything else than repel Tweedledum and embrace Tweedledee.

Well, if we should simply restrict ourselves to the evidences of Democratic success in the East we should be unmoved by the spectacle of a return from the frying pan to the fire. But, . . . there is something extremely encouraging in the fact that the electorate has registered its resentment in such unmistakable terms. . . . The most experienced political correspondents, like Mark Sullivan and David Lawrence, failed to prepare us for the event. . . . Mr. Sullivan, after his trip through the West, was certain that the situation had greatly improved for the Republicans and that they would hold a majority of about forty seats; it was generally agreed that after the ending of the strikes the Republican prospects had brightened. Instead of which we see a vote which has stunned Washington, and gives no ground for the assumption that anything done by the Harding Administration has met with the approval of the electorate. We cannot imagine that the party will be so foolish as to renominate Mr. Harding after this or that he would be willing to accept a second candidacy and risk political extinction such as came to Mr. Taft under similar conditions.

But there are vastly more important results than this to hearten liberals everywhere. The ship subsidy bill[1] has probably been killed by this vote, and so has all possibility of further plundering of the Treasury on a great scale while Mr. Harding is in the White House. If they read the lesson of the ballots aright, Mr. Harding and Mr. Hughes will find no approval whatever of

---

[1] The ship subsidy bill called for sale to private operators on liberal purchase terms of the merchant fleet built by the government for use during the war. In order to keep American shipping competitive with lower cost foreign operators, ship owners were to be granted certain tax exemptions and a subsidy to cover the differential between cost of operations of ships of American registry and foreign vessels. The bill was defeated by a filibuster at the end of the lame duck session of the 67th Congress, February and March, 1923.

their foreign policies. Their indefensible attitude toward Mexico and Haiti, their stupidity in dealing with Russia, their failure to take the lead in bringing the nations together for the economic restoration of Europe, are without the shadow of an indorsement. They will, of course, attribute the defeat to various causes, and it is undeniable that it represents the sum total of a long list of dissatisfactions, but at least they cannot deceive themselves with the assumption that they have popular approval for any one of their policies. Nothing was less effective in the campaign than Mr. Hughes's cold-blooded, "hard-boiled," eleventh-hour defense of the conduct of our foreign affairs. Even more important than all this is the amazing fact that Congress will now be controlled by what the newspapers in their misuse of language call "the radical group." The liberal bloc, for which *The Nation* has been calling for two years past, is here and it is in the saddle. Mr. Harding and his Administration will henceforth have to make terms with Borah, La Follette, Ladd, Norris, and Johnson, with whom will now stand Frazier of North Dakota, Howell of Nebraska, Shipstead of Minnesota, Brookhart of Iowa, and probably on many occasions Reed of Missouri, who, read out of his party convention two years ago by Woodrow Wilson, returns to the Senate perhaps the freest man in it, so far as any party or group allegiance is concerned. The opportunities which rise before this group are almost overwhelming. They can make over the policies of the Republican Party, they can revive all the Progressive enthusiasm of 1912, they can block further blunders by the Harding Administration, they can dictate the next Republican Presidential candidate, or they can discard that party and build a new one, secure in the feeling that they represent the popular desire. For, wherever the progressive or farmer-labor movement appeared in strength, there it was victorious. Oklahoma, Minnesota, North Dakota, Iowa, Nebraska, Colorado, Montana — from all these States comes good news. In every one of them the dominating machine was soundly thrashed, or a blow struck, as in Montana and Colorado, against the big-business domination of those States.

No one can study the returns from this section, and not feel profoundly heartened and chered. An election which puts William E. Sweet into the governorship of Colorado, George W. P. Hunt into that of Arizona, and John J. Blaine back into that of Wisconsin is in itself no mean election.

Never in any such contest was there a greater or more intelligent splitting of tickets, or greater evidence of thought on the part of the voters. In Ohio, for instance, the absurd Presidential boom of the dull and belligerent Senator Pomerene was ended by the election of Congressman Fess, Republican. Then the voters turned around and elected a Democratic Governor. In Nebraska they chose Mr. Bryan's brother, a Democrat, as Governor, and turned out Senator Hitchcock, giving a thoroughly deserved punishment to one who, for party reasons, so completely misrepresented his constituency and abandoned American idealism during the war. In New York City 205,808 votes were cast for Charles P. Steinmetz, the Socialist candidate for State Engineer, although he made no personal campaign and no other Socialist candidate received more than 92,000 votes. But when all is said and done the fact remains that the voters revived a party which ought to be amalgamated with the Republicans, for there is now no shadow of difference between them save in the degree of tariff robbery we should groan under. Like the man who accepted two dollars from the Democrats and five dollars from the Republicans, and then voted for the Democrats because they were the less corrupting, the voters have again chosen the lesser evil, have again voted to punish.

None the less the ferment which the election clearly reveals is a most hopeful augury that the day is not far off when voting may again be *for* constructive policies instead of merely *against* officials or party. A surprising number of free, able, and forward-looking men will control Congress and rule in some of the State capitals. Great economic forces are in play. The deeps are breaking up. What true democrat can feel else than fresh inspiration to the tasks before us?

S T U A R T   A .   R I C E
Farmers and Workers in American Politics
New York: Columbia University Press, 1924, pp. 25–35

CURRENT INDICATIONS OF POLITICAL INSTABILITY

Scattered widely throughout current literature, both popular and serious, is to be found the opinion that traditional party alignments among American voters are disintegrating. Typical of these expressions, and from a source certain to command respect, is the following:

> The differences of principle which parties represent are no longer large enough or well enough defined to be of great interest to the voters; and these voters and their representatives are now concerned with pushing the claims of their several localities or classes. This leaves the field free for the block system to operate.[1]

The evidence for opinions similar to that just quoted is of several sorts: First, the rapid and sweeping reversals of popular favor accorded the major parties during the period since the World War were without parallel in the preceding half century of American elections. This is indicated in the following table, which notes the quadrennial changes in percentage of total votes received by the Republican Party and by the Democratic Party, when each presidential election since 1860 is compared with the preceding one.

The unprecedented "turnover" of votes between 1916 and 1920 is clearly indicated. It has not been equalled since Lincoln, a minority choice in 1860, became a majority president in 1864 with the South disfranchised. Some of the factors that may have played a part in the recent loosening of party ties indicated in Table 1 are the following: (1) Habits of independence created

---

[1] Arthur T. Hadley, *Economic Problems of Democracy*, p. 79.

TABLE 1   Arithmetic Differences in Percentages of Total Vote
Polled at Successive Presidential Elections by Republican
and Democratic Parties[2]

Presidential Elections Compared	Change in Percentage of vote polled by Republican Party	Change in Percentage of vote polled by Democratic Party
1856–1860	6.8	2.2
1860–1864	15.2	2.6
1864–1868	2.4	2.4
1868–1872	2.7	3.3
1872–1876	8.1	6.2
1876–1880	1.0	2.0
1880–1884	.1	.6
1884–1888	.4	.1
1888–1892	5.2	3.0
1892–1896	8.3	.6
1896–1900	.8	.4
1900–1904	4.7	7.9
1904–1908	4.8	5.4
1908–1912	1.0	1.1
1912–1916	1.0	7.3
1916–1920	14.2	15.0

by the insurgent revolt of 1912. It is probable that many
staunch Republicans, under the sway of Theodore Roosevelt's
vigorous personality, broke loose for the first time from their

[2] Editor's note. The following table carries Rice's calculations through
the election of 1968.

Presidential Elections Compared	Change in Percentage of vote polled by Republican Party	Change in Percentage of vote polled by Democratic Party
1920–24	6.3	5.3
1924–28	4.2	12.0
1928–32	18.6	16.6
1932–36	3.1	3.4
1936–40	8.3	6.1
1940–44	1.1	1.3
1944–48	.8	3.8
1948–52	10.0	5.2
1952–56	2.3	2.2
1956–60	7.9	7.7
1960–64	11.0	11.4
1964–68 (approximated)	4.5	18.1

habitual party ties. Having thereby ceased to be "regulars," it seems likely that many such individuals have never since felt themselves as definitely bound as before to a party organization. (2) A majority of the nation's women were enfranchised between 1916 and 1920. In most cases these new voters were without previous party allegiances or voting habits. (3) Situations growing out of the war have confronted many individuals and groups with a conflict between established political habits and the drive of new emotional sympathies or antagonisms. The new war-bred emotions have been strong and likely to prevail. This fact is implied in the widely-held view that President Harding's vast majority in 1920 was the result of the discontent of normally Democratic elements (for example, the Irish) with President Wilson's policies.

Party policies indistinguishable. A second reason advanced for the alleged breakdown of party alignment is that the Republican and Democratic parties possess no distinguishing policies with respect to important public questions. This view is expressed by the assertion that they represent, respectively, "tweedle-dee and tweedle-dum."

This criticism is not wholly accurate. Each of the parties, in state or local affairs, often stands for clean-cut policies on leading issues. But these policies vary among states or sections. In *ensemble,* whenever the issue concerned becomes a matter of nation-wide importance, they cannot be combined into a coherent national policy.

A few illustrations from current events may be cited: The Democratic Party is unmistakably "wet" in New York City, but "dry" in rural Missouri. The Republican Party, with equal certainty, is "dry" in rural New York and "wet" in St. Louis.[3] It cannot be regarded as strange that the attitudes of both parties on the enforcement of the Volstead Act, regarded as a national issue, should be contradictory and obscure.

---

[3] This assertion is based upon the writer's study of legislative roll calls on prohibition legislation in the two states.

Again, the policies of which La Folette is a spokesman have little in common with the policies represented by Senator Lodge. Yet the former seem equally entitled with the latter to the designation of Republican. There is little doubt as to the general character of Wisconsin Republicanism or of New England Republicanism. It is the attempted synthesis of these with various other state and local varieties which renders difficult a characterization of the whole.

With respect to outstanding questions of foreign policy, the difficulties are even more pronounced. At no time since President Wilson's return from Versailles could a safe prediction have been made regarding the attitude of a Senator toward the League of Nations merely from knowledge of his party affiliation. Both parties have pro-League and anti-League wings, just as both have conservative and progressive wings. Each wing has a legitimate and legal claim to represent its party, yet on the specific leading issues, each finds more in common with the corresponding wing of the opposing party than with the opposite wing of its own party.

Congressional "blocs." A third type of evidence indicating the disintegration of the old parties is presented by the appearance of numerous "blocs" in Congress, indicative of corresponding divisions among the voters. These "blocs" for the most part appear to be bi-partisan. Within recent months, New York newspapers have acquainted their readers with a "Farm" bloc, a "Labor" bloc, "Progressive," "Liberal," "Radical" and "People's" blocs, "New England," "New York," "Western," "Middle Western," "Southern" and "Wisconsin" blocs, "Wet," "Dry," "Bonus" and "Mothers" blocs, "Wall Street," "Sugar" and "Oil" blocs, a "Rivers and Harbors" bloc, a "subsidy" bloc and even a "Henry Ford" bloc. A number of these alleged blocs undoubtedly represent little if anything more than a transitory alignment upon a particular vote or issue. Such a use of the term by correspondents, however, testifies to the frequent replacement of party divisions by divisions along other lines, and to the familiarity of the public with the idea of such a replacement.

Evidence like the foregoing has led many statesmen and politicians to the belief that existing party alignments in America are artificial and that a reformation of party issues and party alignments is imminent. For example, Postmaster General New, representing President Harding unofficially, is said to have declared: "I freely admit the division in the Republican ranks but the state of our Democratic adversaries is no better. The trouble from which both parties suffer today is lack of cohesion." [4]

Senator Borah is quoted as saying:

> Political conditions are distressingly unsatisfactory to both political parties. The voter is alarmingly independent. Party lines are shadowy and uncertain. Party leaders seem confused. The rank and file are distrustful. And yet the people are deeply and profoundly interested in public questions and eager for information upon all political problems.[5]

Samuel G. Blythe declares in the most widely-circulated periodical in America:

> We have in this country a new situation in politics, which is a voting population that apparently has cast off the old allegiances and has formed no new ones; that is going somewhere, but has not found out where. We have a political condition entirely at variance with the precedents and preferences of the past two generations; that resembles a general strike against the old parties and old methods.[6]

We should not be too ready to attribute these opinions and the conditions upon which they are based to purely American conditions, for a similar note is often heard from responsible leaders in Great Britain. Mr. Austen Chamberlain believes that "at the present time a large part — I myself believe the larger

---

[4] Quoted in *New York Times*, May 11, 1923, p. 28.
[5] Quoted in *New York Times*, March 22, 1923.
[6] "Presidentitis," *Saturday Evening Post*, March 31, 1923, p. 4.

part — of the electorate belongs to no party," [7] while Lord
Morley refers to "the shattering of parties" and the "multiplica-
tion of endless political schools." [8]

Without regard to causes, and without regard to conditions
in other countries, the evidence and opinions that have been
cited with respect to the instability of parties in America are
sufficient to justify the inquiry which follows. If present alignments are breaking down, as is alleged with some show of
evidence, what is the probability that certain suggested realignments will supplant them? The question of new political parties
is not necessarily involved in this problem. New alliances might
occur as well within the existing major party organizations as
by the formation of new "third" or "fourth" or "fifth" parties.
The problem with which the politician and the sociologist are
concerned is to determine the kind of potential alignments
which now exist spontaneously among the voters, regardless of
party, with respect to various types of issues.

Proposed Farmer-Labor and Other Alignments

At least five different political alliances among major economic groups in the United States have recently been advocated, or are held on one hand or another to be in existence or
in process of formation. These suggested alignments are not
wholly distinct, nor are they for the most part consistent with
each other. They are:

>   Farmer — Labor alliance
>   Farmer — Manufacturer alliance
>   Middle Class — Farmer alliance
>   Middle Class — Capital alliance
>   Middle Class — Farmer — Labor alliance

---

[7] Quoted in editorial, "Unattached Voters," *New York Times*, April 1,
1923.

[8] Quoted in editorial, "Empty Party Bottles," *New York Times*, June 3,
1923.

The results of the state and congressional elections of 1922 in a number of western states were accepted by many observers as evidence of the reality of a farmer-labor alliance. "The discontented farmer and the aspiring laborer have got together," said William Allen White.[9] There seemed to be little evidence in the returns with which to challenge his assertion. The indications of such an alliance seemed strengthened by the special election in Minnesota on July 16, 1923, in which Magnus Johnson, candidate of the Farmer-Labor Party, was elected to succeed the late Senator Knute Nelson.

Some observers, however, have been willing to accept the election data as evidence of coming party realignments, without accepting the alleged farmer-labor alliance as the mold in which realignment would be cast. Col. Robert H. Montgomery, former Comptroller of the United States Shipping Board, maintained in an address a few days after the 1922 election that "both the present parties are a total loss." He asserted that "the manufacturers are a natural and economic ally of the farmers, and an alliance between the farmers and the manufacturers would form the nucleus of new conservative party." "Alliance of the farmers and radicals," he believed, "is ridiculous, a contradiction of the character and history of the American farmer." [10]

Another interpretation of the 1922 election returns was given by Herbert C. Pell, Jr., Democratic State Chairman in New York. Holding that Democratic success was due in great measure to the support of middle class voters, Mr. Pell went on to state:

The middle class, which comprises at least one-quarter of the total population of the country, comprises also about 90 per cent of the brains of the country and it seems to me that the political

[9] From Mr. White's editorial page, "As I See It," *New York Sunday Tribune*, Nov. 12, 1922.

[10] As quoted in accounts of his address before the annual reunion of officials of the War Industries Board, contained in the *New York World* and the *New York Times*, Nov. 12, 1922.

party which appeals to this body of our citizenry will be successful for many years to come.[11]

The relationship of the middle class, so-called, to labor,
farmer and capitalist groups is not easy to comprehend in a single formula. At least two well-defined and contradictory generalizations have been drawn. To a number of writers[12] the
middle class appears to have been caught between Capital and
Labor as between upper and nether mill stones. Labor in particular has profiteered against the nation and hence against the
middle class and the farmers. The latter groups, we infer, have
more in common between them than have middle class and capitalists or middle class and Labor.

Much of the pseudo-economic literature of the Wall Street
news-letter type, on the other hand, identifies the interests of
professional and small business people — the middle-class brain
workers — with the interests of Capital.

There are not lacking those, furthermore, who proclaim the
common interests of industrial workers, farmers and middle
class persons in defending themselves against the exploitation
of Capitalism. Political cooperation between middle and working classes is by these persons regarded as a desirable and possible outcome of economic interests.[13]

Complicating factors in proposed alignments. An examination of any one of these proposed alliances must not overlook
two factors which complicate the inquiry. First of all, each of
the social groups or classes that have been named is in itself

---

[11] Letter from Herbert C. Pell, Jr., Democratic State Chairman in New
York, to Cordell Hull, Democratic National Chairman, quoted by
New York Times, Dec. 18, 1922.

[12] Notably John Corbin in *The Return of the Middle Class,* Scribners,
1922.

[13] For example, New York newspapers have reported efforts of labor
leaders to organize the clerical forces of banks in that city into unions
affiliated with the American Federation of Labor. Affiliation of certain
teachers' organizations with organized labor is evidence of the same sort.

highly diverse. Each is susceptible to sub-classification to an indefinite extent, and each overlaps all of the others at a great many points. The labor world has its aristocracy of skilled tradesmen and its proletariat of unskilled, unorganized manual laborers. Farmers vary in economic status all the way from wealth and ownership of country estates to the tenancy of "croppers" who own little but their own labor. Generalizations with respect to "farmers," "labor" or "capital" must be understood as referring to certain typical situations and there is always danger that the attributes of a sub-group may be mistaken for those of the whole.

In the second place, each of the suggested class alignments is based upon a questionable premise — namely, that political behavior is a resultant of economic interest.

Rational calculation of his own economic interest may sometimes be responsible for the manner in which the individual votes. The writer believes that votes are more often determined by the accumulated background of customs, habits, ideals, judgments of right dealing — what the sociologist terms *mores* — in the mind of each individual voter. It is recognized that each class or group in society possesses *mores* which are particularly its own, as well as those which it shares with other groups entering with it into still larger but less intimate groupings.[14]

Now it is probable that in the long run, *mores* are moulded to fit economic interests. Karl Pearson, for example, presents this probability in extreme form when he maintains: "The civil and moral laws of any given society at a particular time must appear as ultimate results of the struggle for existence between that society and its neighbors." [15] But regardless of this probability, *mores* show a high degree of resistance to economic change. A "lag" of years, or even of decades or centuries may occur between the development of conditions which alter the

---

[14] *Folkways*, Wm. G. Sumner, sec. 46.
[15] *Grammar of Science*, p. 80 ff.

economic interests of a group, and the development of customs and prejudices that best serve it under these changed conditions.[16]

In examining the probability of any possible alignment among the American voters, therefore, we cannot afford to neglect indications of respective economic interests, but we should regard as still more significant any indications of traditional and habitual attitudes on the part of one group toward the other, and toward particular kinds of issues upon which both groups may be called upon to act simultaneously.

When we examine the proposed farmer-labor alliance, a special difficulty arises. We are attempting to compare groups differentiated from the rest of society along different planes. Farmers are those engaged as directors of operations in particular industry. "Labor" represents those engaged in certain occupations, or at certain economic levels, or with certain relations to employers, in a variety of industries. Farmers may be either capitalists or proletarians. The classification is vertical. Labor is made up of proletarians. The classification is horizontal.

Barleycorn's Resurrection as a Big Campaign Issue, *The Literary Digest, 73, June 17, 1922, pp. 12–14*

While there are many months to Election Day, and public opinion is subject to change, recent events have shown that the Prohibition issue will be of importance in the Congressional elections this fall. In fact, well-informed Washington correspondents, such as David Lawrence and W. W. Jermane, told us in April that the greatest of all battles between the "wet" and "dry" forces of America is to be fought during the next few months. And now we find editors from

---

[16] For a lucid analysis of phenomena of "lag" in social evolution, see Ogburn, *Social Change*, pp. 200–213.

all sections of the country agreeing as to the importance
of Prohibition as an issue. Henry Ford's weekly, the *Dear-
born Independent*, and Mrs. Peter Olesen of Minnesota,
Democratic nominee for United States Senator, agree that Prohibition is not a live issue; in the words of Mr. Ford's *Independent*, "it is as dead as slavery." "But what they mean,"
interprets the liberal New York *Telegraph*, "is that they *hope*
Prohibition will not be an issue. The truth is, in Mrs. Olesen's
State it will be *the* issue."

Every day, continues *The Telegraph*, which is frankly
"wet," "evidence accumulates that a referendum is to be had
upon the Volstead Act." And we find this statement echoed
in many of the country's leading papers. The Cleveland *Plain
Dealer*, for instance, which fought for State and national prohibition years ago, admits that "from the standpoint of either
wet or dry, the entire country faces a critical contest." "And
this is as it should be," declares the Boston *Post*, "for in no
better way can public sentiment be ascertained."

"One of the storm centers next fall," we are informed by
the Springfield *Republican*, "will be Massachusetts": "The
referendum on the new State enforcement law, which now
seems assured, will make this State a battle-ground." Others
will be New Jersey, where Governor Edwards is running for
the United States Senate as an avowed "wet," and New York,
where dry-law enforcement is admittedly difficult, and where
the hotels suffer so from hootch-selling restaurants that they
have asked the authorities to enforce the law in the latter places.

It is the announced intention of the wet forces, which are
well organized in at least ten States, to elect a "liberal" Congress and to defeat Congressman Volstead, who, they assert,
is the author of all their woes.[1] To bring about these results
there are some twenty organizations in the field. The dry
forces, on the other hand, with twenty or more organizations

---

[1] Congressman Volstead, author of the federal prohibition enforcement
statute, was defeated in the general election of November, 1922.

and a $2,000,000 fund, are out to keep dry Senators and Representatives in Washington, and to add to their number if possible.

Representatives of eleven States, meeting in Milwaukee at the Anti-Saloon League Conference, united in promising their aid to Congressman Volstead this fall. Nor are Governors of States to be overlooked. State Senator Runyon, of New Jersey, Republican candidate for the nomination for Governor, is to be aided by dry adherents, because he has declared for rigid enforcement of prohibition. But Wisconsin will be the storm center for an attack upon prohibition at the polls, announces Wayne B. Wheeler, general counsel of the Anti-Saloon League, altho stiff fights will be carried on in half a dozen other States. In Wisconsin the wet candidate for Governor, backed by brewery and other wet interests, will find the drys camped upon his trail.

In Texas the League of Women Voters already have obtained the promise of the Senatorial candidate that he will vote against any amendment to the Volstead Act that will legalize light wine and beer. In other States, writes a Washington correspondent of the New York *Times*, "the wet and dry forces are lining up for a campaign that promises to be the best organized and most sturdily contested struggle staged in this country in many years. They are interested in just one thing — whether a candidate is wet or dry. Whether he is a Republican or a Democrat doesn't matter." Continues this writer:

"The wet and dry campaign of 1922 is to be conducted over such a broad field and in sections of the country where the public attitude is so essentially different that it is necessary to visualize the whole political outlook to get at the facts and possibilities. In some sections the struggle will be picturesque, even spectacular, and the issue hard to determine beforehand. In others it will not be much more than a skirmish. It is easy to predict the result in such States as Maine, Vermont, Alabama, South Carolina, Kansas, Nebraska, the two Dakotas,

Iowa and Mississippi. If any wet votes are cast there, it will not take long to count them. But it is a different story in Massachusetts, New Hampshire, Rhode Island, Connecticut, New York, New Jersey, Pennsylvania, Delaware, Maryland, Kentucky, Ohio, Illinois, Indiana, Missouri, Texas, Louisiana, California, Montana, Minnesota, Wisconsin and Tennessee.

"In Illinois the advance guards already have taken up outpost positions. Practically every district in the State will be the scene of a clash, but the big fight is coming in the Peoria District, where Clifford Ireland, the present member, recently was defeated by Edward Hull, who carried the wet banner in the Republican primary.

"Ohio will be another hotly contested sector; the dry forces are against Senator Pomerene (Dem.). Republicans in the Senate agree with their Democratic colleagues that the senior Senator from that State is one of the ablest and cleanest men in public life. But Senator Pomerene has contended that Prohibition was a matter for the States and not the national Government to decide. Altho a teetotaler, in the Senate he voted according to his own best judgment, and because he did so the drys have marked him for defeat.

"In New York and Pennsylvania the wets will contest every inch of ground. They hope to make substantial gains. So far as Prohibition is concerned, the fight will be non-partizan. Where a Democrat is a dry the Anti-Saloon League will support him, and where he is wet, it will seek to accomplish his defeat.

"The fight in New Jersey, as in New York and Pennsylvania, will be hard fought. The drys will back Senator Frelinghuysen against Governor Edwards. There is not a man in the United States whose defeat the Anti-Saloon League would more gladly bring about than that of Governor Edwards. They are going into the struggle against him, determined to make every vote count. It is the same story in the Congressional districts, where the party that nominates a dry will get the Anti-Saloon League support.

"Senator Henry Cabot Lodge of Massachusetts, up for re-election this year, will not find his picture on any of the walls in Prohibition headquarters, for in the last session of Congress Senator Lodge was one of the small group of Senators who fought the so-called 'Volstead, Jr., law.'

"In Rhode Island, where Senator Peter Goelet Gerry hopes to win in November, he will be opposed by the Anti-Saloon League.

"The drys are waiting for Senator du Pont of Delaware to take a stand. They assert that up to now the Senator has not made his position plain. The situation in Delaware, so far as the Senatorship is concerned, will depend to a great extent on the Democratic nominee. The candidate who can pronounce 'Volstead' best will get the dry endorsement. When the Democrats settle on a candidate and Senator du Pont comes off the fence, the dry-and-wet question, so far as it applies to Delaware, will be clear.

"The Maryland outlook is the same as in Delaware, so far as the Senatorial situation is concerned. There will be a battle in every Congressional district. Some of the wettest members of the present Congress are from that State, and all of them are running for reelection.

"Out in Missouri another battle is in the making over the Senate seat of James A. Reed. The drys are fighting Reed for the nomination, and if he wins they will just as bitterly oppose him in the general election.

"Senators La Follette in Wisconsin and Johnson in California also are on the wrong side of dry favor, but even the Anti-Saloon League entertains no serious hope that either can be defeated."

"The 'wet-or-dry' question is the big issue at present," agrees the Baltimore *News*, while the Albany *Knickerbocker Press* advises those who believe in real prohibition to "gird their loins for a battle such as they have never before had to face." For, as the Tulsa *Tribune* observes, "it is becoming plain that there is still some fight left in the wets. In fact, elections in many places this fall will hang on the question whether it is advisable to modify the Volstead Act." Moreover, darkly hints the New York *Evening World*, which is avowedly wet, "there is likely to be a revelation," and the Boston *Post* ventures this political forecast for November: "Possible wet weather in sections where there has been a long dry spell."

CHAPTER 2   Issues,
Alternatives, and
Decisions in 1924

A complex web of fraud and chicanery in the highest levels of government began to unravel shortly before the untimely death of President Harding in August, 1923. Successive Congressional investigations over the next five years uncovered some of the most unseemly scandals in the nation's history. In one of the most blatant of these, Charles Forbes, Harding's appointee to head the well-financed Veterans' Bureau, condemned and sold nearly two million dollars of government supplies at a fraction of their actual cost, collecting a handsome kickback from the purchasers. Forbes' attempt to defend himself, published after his completion of a two year prison sentence, is better testimony to the banality of its author and the men who made up Harding's immediate political circle than it is evidence of the innocence of Charles Forbes. In what was to prove the most spectacular of the scandals of the Harding administration, Secretary of Interior Albert B. Fall was shown to have accepted bribes from the Sinclair and Doheny oil interests as price for his transferring to them leases on the naval oil reserves at Teapot Dome, Wyoming and Elk Hills, California. In the second selection of this chapter, Senator Thomas J. Walsh of Montana, the chairman of the Senate Investigating Committee, details the early stages of the Teapot Dome investigation.

By all expectations, the scandals of the Harding administration should have been a prime issue in the campaign of 1924. They were not. The Republican party obviously wanted to forget them. The Democrats could make little political capital from the scandals because the party could not plead clean hands. Edward L. Doheny had made substantial contributions to Democratic campaign funds; more embarrassing, the Senate investigations revealed that the Democrat's front-running presidential contender as of January, 1924, William G. McAdoo, was being paid a handsome retainer as an attorney for the Doheny interests. McAdoo successfully demonstrated that he had no involvement with the manipulations at Teapot Dome, but he left unanswered what services merited his exorbitant fee. This episode probably sabotaged McAdoo's presidential aspirations and helped neutralize the scandals as a 1924 campaign issue.

Calvin Coolidge, an astute and enterprising politician, discreetly avoided any association with the nefarious activities of the administration he had served as vice-president. He quietly dismissed Harding's attorney general, Harry Daugherty, eliminated the "Ohio Gang" from Washington and projected a personal image of an honesty so pure and rugged that it could not be soiled by any hint of scandal. Combining the advantages of incumbency with control of Republican machines in the states and a policy so evasive that it could win support of avowed Progressives like Senator Borah, Coolidge won the Republican nomination virtually without contest.

Torn asunder by the battle between the rural South and the northern urban machines, the enfeebled Democratic party sagged to its all time low in 1924. This division, which manifested itself in the opposing candidacies of Governor Al Smith of New York and Georgia-born William G. McAdoo as well as in the tactical question of whether to condemn the Ku Klux Klan by name, so deadlocked the New York convention that 104 ballots passed before the delegates could agree upon John W. Davis, a New York corporation lawyer, as a compromise candidate. "Damn Fool Democrats," Arthur Krock labeled the party as he wryly described the circumstances by which the Democrats eliminated themselves from national politics in 1924.

The Progressives, with Senator Robert M. La Follette as their presidential candidate, provided the only spark and the only significant alternatives in the campaign of 1924. The third party represented a coalition of La Follette's personal supporters, some radical farm groups, Socialists and important elements of organized labor. The Progressive platform, which included demands for a popular referendum on any future declaration of war, recall of judicial decisions and stressed La Follette's traditional anti-monopolism, looked backward to Populist type precedents more than it anticipated the complex problems of an urban society. Nevertheless, the political threat of the third party was taken seriously in 1924: the Republican campaign was directed more against the Progressives than against the Democrats.

Three distinguished contributors to a *New Republic* symposium shortly before the balloting found significant alternatives in the decisions soon to be made. Walter Lippmann, never one enamored of illusions, chose to vote against the Republicans, but only where it had practical significance — within the context of the two party system. Chester Rowell, a well-known California editor and a major figure in that state's Progressive movement a decade earlier, shared with a number of political observers the fear of an electoral deadlock. A vote for any other candidate than Coolidge, he argued, could send the election to the House of Representatives. If the House failed to make a decision, the Senate in choosing between vice-presidential candidates could potentially name Charles Bryan, Davis' running mate, the next president. Herbert Croly, author of *The Promise of American Life* (1910) and a founder of the *New Republic*, viewed the decision of 1924 in a different perspective. Only in support for La Follette could Croly find the possibility of initiating the radical social and economic transformation he insisted was necessary.

Despite the impressiveness of Coolidge's victory, the 1924 results show signs of the same political vacillation evident in 1920 and 1922. In most states west of the Mississippi the Progressives replaced the Democrats as the second party. The final selection, an objective and careful analysis of the 1924 results, is particularly concerned with the sources of and significance of the La Follette vote. Its author, Professor Hugh Keenleyside of Syracuse University, was an authority on both United States and Canadian history.

CHARLES R. FORBES

Inside the Harding Administration, *New York World, December 4, 1927, p. 1*

In 1914 Warren G. Harding, Mrs. Harding, Dr. Charles E. Sawyer and Mrs. Sawyer came to the Hawaiian Islands. Harding was then Senator-elect from Ohio and was taking a rest after a vigorous campaign. . . . I was then the Commissioner of Public Works in the Territory. . . . I was with Harding during his entire stay . . .

During this association Harding expressed to me what he hoped to achieve as United States Senator. He remarked that he wanted to represent not only Ohio but all of the United States. The comment made a lasting impression on me. It exhibited to me what seemed a splendid Americanism and it forcibly reminded me of the selfish political ambitions of many others.

I recall that as we sat at the rim of a crater, looking down into the seething mass of molten lava, he said: "This is God's work and He alone can quiet the flame." He was truly spiritual.

He told me much about himself, his family, his home life and his hopes. He saw a great need for progressive legislation. He

was interested particularly in an American merchant marine,
child welfare, Federal support for education throughout the
United States and especially in the South, national defense and
less Federal interference with the prerogatives of the States.
He spoke feelingly of a man's responsibilities to his home and he
believed implicitly in the sanctity of one's own castle. During
this period of our early acquaintance I formed an opinion of this
lovable character that after years has been steadily deepened.

In the following session of Congress Harding became a member of the Upper House. His critics have said that he achieved
little as a Senator; that he was a mediocre type of statesman.
It is true that he was not bombastic, but he worked earnestly
with his colleagues for such legislation as he thought would
benefit his country. He was truly a Senator of America. He
had not completed his first term when he was elected President
of the United States.

I propose now, from a store of memories of the Harding
Administration, to throw light upon some of the men and
events of that period. I will be very happy if I can be the
means of removing any stigma from the memory of a dead
friend. He possessed extreme tenderness, abounding generosity
and an unwavering faith in mankind. In private life these
beautiful characteristics endeared him to the hearts of men.
In public life, they proved, unhappily, to be elements of weakness — a weakness that would have destroyed him had he
lived. I propose to show how Harding was betrayed by some
of those in whom he had reposed implicit faith. It is not a
pleasant story, but it is a story which, in the light of recent
attacks upon his memory, needs to be told in his defense.

My title to speak of him and his Administration is based on
an intimacy that endured from the time of his visit to Honolulu
to the hour of his death in San Francisco.

It is claimed that Harry Daugherty was responsible for Harding's candidacy for the Presidency. This is incorrect. The
real sponsor and advocate was Florence Kling Harding, his
strong-minded and ambitious wife. It is true that Harry early

became interested in Harding's candidacy, as did the writer, but it is also true that there were others who had long prior to this time urged him to enter the field. In fact, his candidacy was discussed at a conference with Theodore Roosevelt in the office of the *Outlook* in New York City in 1915. I was present. Notwithstanding the differences of opinion between these two men, Roosevelt exhibited a lively interest in Harding and a genuine fondness for him. I am convinced that, next to Major Gen. Leonard Wood, Harding was Roosevelt's choice fo the Republican nomination in 1920. . . .

As Harding's campaign took form Daugherty became his pre-convention manager. Any and all instructions concerning Harding's campaign, in which I took part, were received from Daugherty, except for such personal matters as were intrusted to me by the candidate himself. Harry continued in this capacity until the nomination was made when Will Hays took command. . . .

There is no doubt that Harry Daugherty was the evil genius of the Harding administration and that the country merchant, Jess Smith, Harry's handy man, who killed himself May 30, 1923, when faced with exposure of his speculations, was an honest man until he came under the malign influence of Daugherty.

[*New York World* Editor's Note. Jess Smith, the "mystery man" of the Harding administration, was found dead in Harry Daugherty's apartment in the Wardman Park Inn. Daugherty was a guest at the White House at the time. . . . The Coroner returned a verdict of suicide, and Smith's friends attributed his act to worry over ill health. It has been charged by Senator Heflin on the floor of the Senate and has been insinuated by others that Smith was murdered because he knew too much.]

While Harry Daugherty was busy with the reorganization of the Department of Justice, I discussed with him the appointment of several judges in Hawaii . . . He told me that I should get in touch with Howard Mannington, who then had

headquarters in the Lafayette Hotel in Washington. Mannington, like Jess Smith, was not an official of the Government. He
was one of the Ohio gang whom Daugherty had brought to
Washington.

While I was discussing the Judgeships with him, Mannington, to my amazement, produced the Department of Justice
file on all the aspirants for the Judgeships in Hawaii and told
me that Daugherty had intrusted the selection of a number of
the appointees to him. . . . It seemed to me then, as it seems
now, a shocking thing that Mannington, with no official cre-
dentials from the Government, should have exercised the influence that he did in the making of appointments to the Federal bench.

I recall that when I was talking with Mannington . . . Jim
Darden came in. Darden, who was from the South, was then a
textile operator, and later, I believe, became an oil man. It may
be interesting to relate how Darden came into the picture. He
met Harding through Daugherty and made a $5000 contribu-
tion to the Harding pre-convention campaign. I recall this
contribution very well. This money was turned over to Dr.
Sawyer, who bought $5000 worth of whiskey with it. The
liquor was stored at Dr. Sawyer's White Oak Sanitarium, at
the Marion Club and at Harding's residence. Whenever the
supply ran low at the Harding house it was replenished from
one of the other depots.

During Albert B. Fall's sojourn there it was necessary to
keep the larder at the Harding home well supplied. But he
was not the only one who drew upon it; indeed the $5000
worth of whiskey was far from sufficient to quench the thirst
of the office seekers who descended upon Marion. I don't
want it to be inferred that Mr. Harding himself was dispensing
the liquor. It was kept in the bottom section of the sideboard
in the Harding dining room.

[*New York World* Editor's Note. Darden was head of an
oil company which had a claim on Teapot Dome, and which
moved a drilling rig onto the reserve about the time that Fall

leased it to Harry Sinclair. Fall sent a squad of Marines . . . to eject the Darden outfit.

In describing before the Walsh committee of the Senate how he received his orders from Fall, Capt. Shuler testified that Fall told him there had been a talk that morning between Fall and President Harding, at which Fall informed the President of his intentions. Fall said the President objected, declaring that Darden was his friend and had contributed $5000 to his campaign fund. Fall quoted himself as replying:

"Well, Mr. President, your friend is a low down ———— ————," to which Fall said the President rejoined: "I suppose he was all of that when we got his check, but it didn't prevent us from using the money."]

Howard Mannington moved from the Lafayette Hotel to the Little Green House on K Street. Thereafter all my business with him was transacted in the small house belonging to Ned McLean, publisher of the Washington Post, adjacent to the old Shoreham Hotel. Jess Smith and Daugherty lived there. In this little house . . . I spent most of one night in June, 1921, when Harry Daugherty was going through the contents of hundreds of criminal files for the purpose of selecting men for pardon. I saw him and helped him. I didn't know what it was all about until Harry told me. . . .

As Harry was going through the bootlegger file he remarked that the President approved clemency for bootleggers only in exceptional cases, but I noted the strange fact that the great majority of those that Daugherty selected for clemency were bootleggers. I drew his attention to this fact, and he remarked: "These are the exceptional cases."

. . . . I want to admit frankly that I was a drinking man and that my best liquor was obtained from the vault of Harry Daugherty's quarters in the little McLean house. All the liquor there was delivered under the protection of the Department of Justice.

. . . . You may be sure that Harry overlooked no precautions, for it was in this little McLean house and the Little

Green House on K Street that he and his clique plotted their treachery to the people and the President.

Daugherty wrote me . . . that he would not accept a Cabinet position if it were offered to him, as it was necessary for him to engage in something that would permit him to recoup his finances. From what I saw of the operations of Daugherty, I have no doubt that his appointment as Attorney General made that possible.

There can be no doubt whatsoever that Harry Daugherty was familiar with every action of his henchman, Jess Smith. On one occasion I saw in Jess Smith's office in the Department of Justice Building $75,000 in $1000 bills. The wind blew them off a table onto the floor and I helped to pick them up. Jess said they belonged to Daugherty.

Jess called upon me frequently concerning affairs of the Government and he always stressed the importance of action because Harry Daugherty had sent him. In every instance, I would either telephone to Harry or call on him at his office, and I always found him in full knowledge of the message Jess had delivered. . . .

Another incident comes to my memory in this connection. . . . I received a phone call from Harry Daugherty, who asked me to come over to the Department of Justice. I went over there and Harry said that he was interested in having me buy for the Veterans' Bureau a certain site in Boston belonging to the Elks. Jess himself was a big Elk.

The price that Harry named . . . was $150,000. I was later informed by a member of the Elks' Club, which owned this property, that it could be had for $20,000. I took the matter up with the President, went to Boston and examined the site. On the strength of my report the President remarked that the property should not be acquired, and it was not acquired. I am not quite certain what Daugherty's game was in this instance, but if he had his way the property would have been unloaded on the Government at a price far in excess of its real value. . . .

In order to lead up to certain events which I now wish to

describe I must go back to a time shortly after the President's inauguration. I had returned from Wasington to Tacoma. While there I received a letter from President Harding asking me to come back to Washington and see him. I left for Washington shortly thereafter, in April, 1921, and upon arrival at Union Station called the President on the telephone.

He asked me to come over right away, telling me to enter the White House by the back way and come into the Cabinet room. I did so. He explained that he wanted me to accept the Governorship of Alaska. I told him that I was not keen to go to Alaska and that the only job in the government that I was interested in was a place on the Shipping Board. . . .

The President pressed the Governorship of Alaska upon me. At his request I went to call the next day on Secretary Fall of the Interior Department, which has jurisdiction over Alaska. While we were discuing the Governorship he called my attention to a large industrial map of Alaska on the wall. He explained to me the wonderful resources of the country and we discussed coal, gold and oil. He pointed with a pencil to the desirable locations for development. He appeared enthusiastic over the possibilities for development and keenly interested in the selection of Governor.

I left him with the understanding that we would meet again the following afternoon. I went back to the White House and reported my interview with Fall, telling the President of Fall's invitation to see him the next day. . . .

After the dinner the President and I went to his library and discussed Alaskan and Shipping Board matters. He asked me if I would care to go to Peru as Ambassador if I did not accept the Alaskan post. I was with him until midnight. To my great surprise, when I returned to the hotel I was met by several men who congratulated me upon my appointment as Governor of Alaska. I said that I had not been appointed. They seemed to be well informed and were eager to accompany me and take part in my inauguration. Among them were a Mr. McBride, the Republican National Committeeman for Alaska, and a

Mr. Ryan, who was interested in mines up there. Their discussion with me was about Alaskan resources, and I concluded that they had been sent to find out where I would stand — hitched or otherwise — with regard to the exploitation of the territory.

I became more firmly convinced of this the following day. In the morning George Christian, the President's secretary, called me and said the President wanted me to take luncheon with him. The President there informed me that Fall had called upon him and had stated that, inasmuch as I had served in public office . . . under a Democratic regime, he (Fall) might be criticized if he supported me for the Governorship. This seemed to me pretty thin, especially as Fall himself had at one time been a Democrat. I told the President that I had not liked the form of Fall's cross-examination. The President said: "Don't let that worry you. If you want to be Governor I will send your name up to the Senate tomorrow." I replied that I did not want either that place or the Ambassadorship to Peru.

I went to New York and attended a dinner given for me by Frank Munsey at the Yale Club. Late that night I received a telephone call from the White House inviting me back to Washington. On my arrival early the next morning I was met by Dr. Sawyer, who said the President wanted me to bring my bag up to the White House, as he had some business to talk over with me. We went up there in the White House car which had brought Dr. Sawyer to the station. The President met me in his office and said: "I have a big job for you and I want you to take it and be ready to start as soon as possible. I want you to take the Bureau of War Risk Insurance." I said that I knew nothing about insurance. He replied that that was an advantage. He told me to go over there and walk through the building and let him have my impressions. I did this. I then asked the President to give me a night in which to think it over. He said, "Why do that?" Whereupon he rang for Secretary Mellon to come over.

He introduced me to him as the new Director of the War Risk Insurance Bureau. After a few minutes more conversation I went over to Mr. Mellon's private office and was sworn in. . . .

My first visitor after my appointment was Dr. Sawyer, the President's physician, and his first utterance to me was: "Now let's do some real work." I inquired what work he wanted done and he said that he wanted to kick out Dr. Haven Emerson, Medical Director of the bureau, and Dr. Salmon, a nonpaid member of the White Committee, which had been appointed by Secretary Mellon to recommend sites for hospitals. I said: "Doctor, I don't know those gentlemen and you surely don't expect me to take such drastic action without making inquiries." He said that Emerson had insulted him and he made a similar ridiculous charge against Dr. Salmon. I told him that his charges were preposterous and I continued Dr. Emerson as head of the medical division. . . .

Immediately I sensed a pitfall into which I would eventually stumble unless I watched my step. From then on and during my entire tenure of office Dr. Sawyer, the President's personal physician, whom the President made a Brigadier General, sought to dominate the bureau and its employees and to destroy my policies. He carried falsehoods to the President and sought to locate hospitals in a way that would be advantageous to his own interests. A homeopath himself, he sought to have homeopaths replace allopaths. He established a stool-pigeon system within the bureau and in other departments of Government as well. He was a vain, strutting little creature and fancied that he had a great attraction for women. He held himself out to be the personal representative of the President and he spoke with a great show of authority when asserting his position.

When the Veterans' Bureau, which took over the work of the War Risk Insurance Bureau, was created, the President selected me as Director and on the following day I was confirmed by the Senate. About this time Sawyer brought about the organization of the board known as the Federal Hospitalization Board.

He was named Chairman and I Vice Chairman. The purpose of the board was to recommend methods of hospital treatment and of hospital construction and to act as advisers to the Director of the Veterans' Bureau. Sawyer immediately had himself installed in the new Veterans' Bureau Building with a corps of clerks who had little to do. He also maintained quarters in the State, War and Navy Building, where his stool pigeons reported daily to him and received their orders from him.

I found that my first impressions of this man were accurate. He was responsible for the destruction of more good in the departments of Government than any other man I know. He was constantly prying into the affairs of the army and navy. Had he lived and been continued in authority, I believe that the United States Public Health Service would today be a disorganized mob instead of the efficient organization that it is. . . .

In his efforts to crush the Public Health Service, Sawyer enlisted the support of an Assistant Director of the Veterans' Bureau who was seeking promotion in the Reserve Corps of the Public Health Service. This man engineered the theft of a number of bottles of whiskey from the depot at Perryville and as part of a plot to "frame" me placed them in a closet in my home in my absence from the city. On my return home I found what had been done and I demanded that he remove the whiskey forthwith. He went to my house . . . and took away the liquor. I reported the affair to the President and sought the Assistant Director's dismissal, only to find that Sawyer had influenced the President to retain him. . . .

I do not know whether Harding knew Harry Sinclair prior to his inauguration. I do know that he met Sinclair at the White House and that Sinclair was an overnight guest there on several occasions. My first knowledge of this was in the summer of 1921. A card party was contemplated. Not knowing that it had been called off, I went to the White House at the appointed hour. Arriving there I said to the President: "Where are the rest of your guests?" He replied that it had become necessary to cancel the evening's pleasure because of a business matter requiring his attention. "But," he said, don't go away. Come to the library and let's have a chat."

About 9:30 P.M. Sinclair arrived and was announced. I had never met the gentleman. I left the library and passed Mr. Sinclair in the hall as the President approached him. I joined Mrs. Harding at the west end of the living room and spent two hours talking with her about people and affairs in Washington. Mrs. Harding inquired if I had met Mr. Sinclair and I replied that I had not. I did not know the purpose of Sinclair's visit.

The postponed poker party was held the following evening in the library of the White House. It was like many similar parties which were held there. We played at a rectangular table in the north end of the room. On this particular occasion the President sat at one end and Will Hays, who was then the Postmaster General, at the other. The others there were Albert Lasker, at that time Chairman of the Shipping Board; Harry Daugherty, Ned McLean, Mrs. McLean and Mrs. Harding. Mrs. Harding did not play — she often sat with us at poker games, but never played. I remember that it was very hot and Albert Lasker took his coat off, displaying red suspenders two inches wide. I won $397 and Will Hays won. The losers all paid up promptly.

During the game Ned McLean announced that Jack Johnson, the prize fighter, was to be discharged from the Federal Penitentiary at Leavenworth, and either Ned or Albert Lasker exclaimed, "Why his old mother used to work for me and he has a fine of $1000 hanging over him and can't pay it." Ned McLean said: "Albert, I'll give $500 and you give $500 and we will pay his fine." The President spoke up: "Don't let that worry you, I'll remit the fine," and the game went on.

Records at the Department of Justice show the $1000 fine assessed against Johnson was not paid. . . .

The President was a good card player. He had a feeling for cards and he sat in numerous games at the White House, the

McLean home and on the Mayflower. . . . The last time I played poker on the Mayflower the players were the President, Harry Daugherty, Gen. Pershing, Gen. Charles G. Dawes, now Vice President Dawes, Harry New and myself. It was a nice little session and I won. Pershing also won. The Boss lost.

I recall the showing of the Dempsey-Carpentier fight film at the country home of Ned McLean. There were many guests there from official life, including the President, and of course, we all knew that the law had been broken in the transportation of the film to Washington. It was amusing to see how every one who was there joined the purity squad when the news leaked out that the film had been shown.

A few days after the visit of Harry Sinclair to the White House, which I have referred to, I dropped into the White House unofficially. I didn't go upstairs. Ike Hoover, the chief usher, called for Mrs. Harding and she came down. Her first greeting was: "Have you heard any comments about Harry Sinclair?" "No," I replied, "what about it?" Mrs. Harding said: "Why, nothing," and the subject was dropped.

On Christmas Day in 1921, I had a telephone call from Mrs. Carolyn Votaw, the President's sister, who was at the White House: "Come on over," she said. "Warnie wants to talk to you." She always called the President "Warnie." I went over and found the President sitting all alone in his office and evidently very depressed. He said, "Merry Christmas," reached into a right-hand drawer of his desk, pulled out a plug of Piper Heidstock and took a chew. He got up and looked out on the White House garden, and said, "Help yourself to a cigaret."

I took a cigaret, lit it, and went over and stood beside him. He said: "This is a hell of a Christmas." I asked him what was the matter and he replied: "Everything is the matter." I gathered from his mutterings that things were not all right with him in his domestic life. In this same conversation the President told me that there were things going on in the public business that he didn't approve — but that he was helpless to stop them.

Later that day I met old Sawyer, who was there every morning to feel the President's pulse and to advise a new brand of pills. Sawyer laughed and said: "My God, they had a hell of a row this morning." He meant the President and his wife.

One night I went out with the President to the rear lawn of the White House, and he cried. There had been a recital that night. After it was over I went upstairs. I met Major Brooks, the colored valet, and he asked me if the President was coming up. I told him yes. Mrs. Harding then came up and said, "Brooks, mix the Colonel a cocktail." Brooks, I might add, was famous for his cocktails. The President came up and joined us. Mrs. Harding went on to her bedroom and the President and I went downstairs and out onto the balcony overlooking the garden.

"Let's take a walk," he said, and we walked down to about the centre of the grounds and sat on a bench, and he told me how unhappy he was and how empty his life had been. "You know something of it," he said. He wept. We went back to the veranda and sat down and I engaged him in conversation about the Ship Subsidy Bill that Lasker was sponsoring. I was with him until about midnight. He was the most unhappy man that I have ever known.

It was perhaps a month after Sinclair's first visit when he was there again, and the day after his second visit President Harding told me that the Interior Department was reaching out for a lot more territory. I asked him what he meant by "territory," and he told me that he meant certain oil lands. I said: "What's the idea?" My mind went back to the fact that at one time I had owned a few shares in a company controlled by Capt. William Matson, the Honolulu Oil Company, which operated in the Buena Vista Reserve in California. So I said to the President: "By the way, Mr. President, I believe that it was in 1916 on my way from Honolulu to Washington to appear before the Rivers and Harbors Committee, that Capt. Matson asked me to sound out Josephus Daniels on his attitude toward the removal of oil from the Buena Vista Reserve." I might add that on that

occasion Harding, then a Senator, gave me a letter of introduction to Daniels, then Secretary of the Navy, remarking that he
was a "splendid fellow" and that I would like him. When I
mentioned the reserves to Daniels he said: "I'll seal them up
so tight as a drum. That oil belongs to the navy."

This incident came back to me when President Harding
brought up the subject of naval oil. I said to him: "If the oil
is to be used for naval purposes, why let the Interior Department administer it?" He said: "It doesn't sound proper, does
it?" He added that many naval officers were opposed . . .
I said to him: "Are you sure Dr. Sawyer hasn't advised you?"
He looked at me and smiled. . . .

In my opinion President Harding acted against his better
judgment when he signed the famous executive order transferring the control of the oil reserves from the Navy to the
Interior Department. He was very easy to impress. Fall put it
over on him. Denby was an innocent party. He was an honorable man and a faithful public servant but the wool was pulled
over his eyes.

Harry Daugherty has said that the Teapot Dome issue was
never brought to his notice for an opinion as to its legality.
He has said that he knew nothing of the making of this
lease. . . .

Daugherty knew all about it. He stayed out of the oil case
as far as he could because he knew it was rotten and he was
not anxious to give an opinion on the issue. Because of his full
knowledge of the oil situation it was his duty as the Attorney
General of the United States to demand that he be allowed to
examine the lease. President Harding would not have stood in
the way of such an examination. I repeat that Harry Daugherty
knew everything that went on in connection with the leasing
of the oil reserves.

One evening in the President's office shortly after the signing
of the Teapot Dome lease the oil matter came up again and the
President said: "Well, I guess there will be hell to pay. But
these fellows seem to know what they are doing."

. . . . I am satisfied that President Harding did not profit by the oil transactions and did not suspect Fall of profiting by them. . . .

It might be of interest in this connection, as showing the political pressure which was constantly being put upon the [Veteran's] Bureau, to name some of those who at one time or another sought favors for their districts. Frank Mondell of Wyoming, the Republican floor leader of the House, wanted money spent generously at Fort McKenzie, Wyo. Senator Lodge was insistent that a hospital be established in the metropolitan area of Boston. Senator Hale of Maine urged the location of a vocational school at Bangor, Me. Congressman Summers of Washington wanted further extensions made to a hospital at Walla Walla. Senator Spencer clamored for a hospital at St. Louis and Senator Wadsworth for one in Upper New York State.

The Minnesota delegation in Congress demanded additional hospital facilities in that State. Senator Ashurst pressed for a hospital in Phoenix, in his home state of Arizona, and became very bitter against me when his request was denied. Senator Frelinghuysen put in a similar bid for New Jersey. Senator Sutherland wanted me to buy a hotel in West Virginia and turn it into a hospital. Senator Harreld wanted a hospital in Oklahoma. And there were scores of others with similar requests. Everybody who had a wooden nutmeg to sell tried to unload it on the Veterans' Bureau.

My conviction at Chicago was obtained as a result of a single contract. This was for the construction of the foundations of the hospital at Northampton, Mass., the home of President Coolidge. The land had been donated by the town of Northampton and the location of the hospital there had been urged upon the bureau by the Chamber of Commerce at Northampton with the indorsement of Mr. Coolidge, then the Vice President. The proposition was clean from first to last.

I have been severely criticized for failing to testify at my trial . . . I could not take the stand in my own behalf without creating a lot of unhappiness in the lives of others who were victims of Elias H. Mortimer's villainy.

I felt, moreover, that my innocence had been fully proved by evidence which showed that I was not even in the Drake Hotel at the time when Mortimer claimed he there paid me a bribe of $5000. Mortimer charged that I gave him advance information relating to sites where hospitals were to be built but he never produced the list which he alleged contained this information. Mortimer's evidence was wholly uncorroborated. I was convicted solely on the evidence of a man who said on the witness stand that he would do anything to put me in the penitentiary, even if he had to go there himself.

It has been said that President Harding demanded my resignation and that we had a violent row at the White House. I can produce a witness who is still in the Government service and who overheard the conversation between us. It was extremely friendly. When I took office I had asked to be allowed to withdraw after a year. I voluntarily tendered my resignation to take effect Jan. 1, 1923. I can produce in the President's own handwriting his memorandum to me changing the date of my resignation to March 1, 1923.

I am aware that there were those who were constantly trying to destroy our friendship, and for no other reason than jealousy. Gen. Sawyer was the most active of these. They never succeeded. Prior to the President's departure for Alaska and after I had left the Veterans' Bureau I was a luncheon guest at the White House. I urged the President to abandon his proposed trip, saying that in my opinion he was undertaking a most hazardous journey. He said he had gone too far with his plans to draw back. He asked me if I would be on the Pacific Coast on his arrival there and I told him I would.

I was there when he arrived at Oakland and I stopped at the Palace Hotel in San Francisco where he and his party had rooms. Our companionship endured to the last....

Warren G. Harding was a much misunderstood man. If he erred in the administration of his high office, it was solely out

of an excess of loyalty to friends whom the world now knows
to have been faithless. I am confident that before he departed
for Alaska he had begun to suspect what these men had done
to him and to the country, and that this suspicion contributed
to his untimely death.

THOMAS J. WALSH
The True History of Teapot Dome, *The Forum, LXXII, July
1924, pp. 1–12*

In the spring of 1922 rumors reached parties interested that a
lease had been or was about to be made of Naval Reserve No. 3
in the State of Wyoming, — popularly known, from its local
designation, as the Teapot Dome. This was one of three great
areas known to contain petroleum in great quantity which had
been set aside for the use of the Navy, — Naval Reserves No. 1
and No. 2 in California by President Taft in 1912, and No. 3 by
President Wilson in 1915. The initial steps toward the creation of these reserves, — the land being public; that is, owned
by the Government, — were taken by President Roosevelt,
who caused to be instituted a study to ascertain the existence
and location of eligible areas, as a result of which President
Taft in 1909 withdrew the tracts in question from disposition
under the public land laws. These areas were thus set apart
with a view to keeping in the ground a great reserve of oil
available at some time in the future, more or less remote, when
an adequate supply for the Navy could not, by reason of the
failure or depletion of the world store, or the exigencies possibly of war, be procured or could be procured only at ex-
cessive cost; in other words to ensure the Navy in any exigency
the fuel necessary to its efficient operation.

From the time of the original withdrawal order, private interests had persistently endeavored to assert or secure some
right to exploit these rich reserves, the effort giving rise to a

struggle lasting throughout the Wilson administration. Some
feeble attempt was made by parties having no claim to any of
the territory to secure a lease of all or a portion of the reserves, but in the main the controversy was waged by claimants asserting rights either legal or equitable in portions of the
reserves antedating the withdrawal orders, on the one hand,
and the Navy Department on the other. In that struggle Secretary Lane was accused of being unduly friendly to the
private claimants, Secretary Daniels being too rigidly insistent
on keeping the areas intact. President Wilson apparently supported Daniels in the main in the controversy which became
acute and Lane retired from the Cabinet, it is said, in consequence of the differences which had thus arisen.

The reserves were created, in the first place, in pursuance of
the policy of conservation, the advocates of which, a militant
body, active in the Ballinger affair, generally supported the
attitude of Secretary Daniels and President Wilson.

They too became keen on the report of the impending lease
of Teapot Dome. Failing to get any definite or reliable information at the departments, upon diligent inquiry, Senator Kendrick of Wyoming introduced and had passed by the Senate
on April 16, 1922, a resolution calling on the Secretary of the
Interior for information as to the existence of the lease which
was the subject of the rumors, in response to which a letter was
transmitted by the Acting Secretary of the Interior on April
21, disclosing that a lease of the entire Reserve No. 3 was made
two weeks before to the Mammoth Oil Company organized by
Harry Sinclair, a spectacular oil operator. This was followed
by the adoption by the Senate on April 29, 1922 of a resolution
introduced by Senator La Follette directing the Committee
on Public Lands and Surveys to investigate the entire subject
of leases of the naval oil reserves and calling on the Secretary
of the Interior for all documents and full information in relation to the same.

In the month of June following, a cartload of documents
said to have been furnished in compliance with the resolution

was dumped in the committee rooms, and a letter from Secretary Fall to the President in justification of the lease of the Teapot Dome and of leases of limited areas on the other reserves was by him sent to the Senate. I was importuned by Senators La Follette and Kendrick to assume charge of the investigation, the chairman of the committee and other majority members being believed to be unsympathetic, and assented the more readily because the Federal Trade Commission had just reported that, owing to conditions prevailing in the oil fields of Wyoming and Montana, the people of my State were paying prices for gasoline in excess of those prevailing anywhere else in the Union.

In the letter of Secretary Fall the course taken was said to have been required by the fact that wells in the adjacent Salt Creek field were draining the oil from the Teapot Dome area. As this theory was disputed, two geologists were employed by the committee to make a study of the ground during the summer of 1923, and the committee, on the incoming of their report, entered, on October 22, 1923, upon the inquiry with which it was charged. I had meanwhile caused to be made a somewhat careful but by no means complete examination of the mass of documents furnished the committee by the Department of the Interior, and went into a laborious study of the exhaustive reports made by the experts, much of it of a highly technical character. I undertook a critical analysis of the lease itself and of the lengthy letter of Secretary Fall to the President, and prepared to interrogate him on the stand concerning features of both, with the purpose of bringing out what I conceived to be fatal vices in the one and misrepresentations and weaknesses in the other.

Incidental to this part of the preparation it was necessary to make a careful study of the acts of Congress of February 25, 1920, and June 4, 1920, of the so-called Overman act, and the statutes touching contracts by the executive departments generally and by the Navy Department specifically. A somewhat intimate familiarity with the laws in relation to the disposition of the public domain and the procedure before the Department of the Interior in connection therewith lightened the task of preparation.

Concurrently with the prosecution of the work outlined, I addressed letters to all journals which had exhibited any special interest in the subject either at the time or since publicity was given to the execution of the Teapot Dome lease, asking for such information as they might be able to give me or for the sources of the statements of facts made in articles appearing in their columns on the subject.

The reports of the experts gave not a little support to the contention that drainage to an appreciable, if not a very considerable, extent was taking place from the Teapot Dome into the Salt Creek wells, contrary to the view expressed by some, whose opinions were entitled to respect, that owing to the geological conditions such a result could not ensue. This was unfortunate because from the first it was recognized that there would be some migration of oil across the boundary line of Naval Reserve No. 3 which was purposely made to embrace an area beyond what was believed to be the separate Teapot Dome structure, that the oil in it might be safe.

The Geological Survey had reported that some drainage was taking place and had recommended that the situation be met by drilling a row of line wells along the relatively narrow common boundary. The propriety of leasing the whole nine thousand acres should have been mooted rather than the question of whether any drainage was taking place or to be apprehended. However, the reports of the experts submitted at the first day's session were decidedly favorable to the leasing so far as they went, and in the popular mind, if one may so speak, when general indifference to the whole subject was the rule, they went the whole length, it being supposed that the only question involved was geological.

The effect of the reports was heightened by the grossest misrepresentation concerning their import, put out by one of the great news agencies, subsequently asserted by it and probably truly, through the error of a careless reporter. A member of the committee gave out the statement that the inquiry would terminate within a day or two. Apathetically a few reporters listened in the succeeding sessions to the tedious presentation of extracts from official documents and publications setting out the need of an oil reserve, of the wisdom of maintaining a great supply in the ground, and reciting the story of the efforts of private interests to secure a foothold within the reserves. Secretary Fall being called to the stand, it was disclosed that hardly had the new administration been installed when the determination was arrived at to transfer the administration of the reserves from the Navy Department to which it had been confided by Congress, because it was believed that department was friendly to their preservation, to the Interior Department, suspected of being disposed to tolerate their exploitation, and an order making the transfer bearing date May 30, 1921, over the signature of President Harding, was brought to light. No one now seriously contends that the President had any authority to issue such an order, which, however, at the time of its promulgation, notwithstanding that fact and its evil augury, evoked little attention, though the significance of it was not lost on the watchful leaders of the conservation movement, particularly as Secretary Fall was known from his record in the Senate to be far from friendly to the conservation policy.

No one seemed willing to assume any wrong in or even to criticise the acts of the new administration, buttressed by that seven million majority and guided by the "best minds." Some little dent in the complacent confidence of the public was made at the time the lease was made through the speeches of Senators Kendrick and La Follette, who called attention to the significant fact that its execution indicated a departure from the settled policy of the Government; that it reversed the result of the struggle that had been carried on throughout the preceding administration; that it was made pursuant to negotiations prosecuted in secret and without competitive biddings. But the listlessness of the public was but little disturbed.

Interest flared fitfully later on when Sinclair declared before a Senate Committee that he expected to make $100,000,000 out of the lease, but it was at a low ebb when the hearings began and the reports of the experts chilled whatever there remained. Nevertheless the reversal of the policy to which general adherence had been given, the secrecy which attended the negotiations, the effort to keep from the public information that the lease had been executed, cast about the transaction a suspicion which my study of the facts had heightened until it had passed to conviction. This was strengthened by the examination of Fall and the disclosures made in connection with his testimony. It might be entertaining did time or space permit to specify these in detail. Misstatements of fact in the letter to the President were not infrequent, but more persuasive with me was the total disregard of the plain provisions of the law, and the utterly untenable arguments made to sustain the action that was taken.

To illustrate: twice in letters to the President upon inquiry from Senators, Fall justified the executive order upon the Overman act and the acts of February 25 and June 4, 1920. Confronted with the Overman act he was compelled to admit that by its plain language it had no application. He could find nothing in either of the other acts to justify his reference to them and then fell back on some vague authority arising from the general scheme of our government. He made a futile effort to find some ground for the provision in the contract authorizing the use of the oil to pay the cost of constructing great storage tanks, pursuant to a program of the navy, which contemplated the construction of public works without authorization by Congress, involving an expenditure mounting up to $102,000,000. He took great credit to himself for sagaciously inserting in the lease that the pipe line to be constructed by Sinclair should be a common carrier, which the interstate commerce law made it without any stipulation to that effect. He reiterated the assertion made in his letter to the President that he considered himself the guardian of important military secrets of the Government in connection with the leases which he would, under no circumstances, reveal, plainly intimating that those who were trying to pry into the affair were lacking in loyalty and wanting in that fine sense of duty to country by which he was actuated, recalling, to me at least, that cynical saying of Dr. Johnson that patriotism is the last refuge of a scoundrel. He was voluble to a degree.

There followed other witnesses, mainly attachés of the department, who testified about drainage and kindred matters when the committee suspended on November 2 to resume on November 30, the case being made as to the legality of the leases, which no one in either house of Congress rose to defend on the resolution to begin suit to annul them, and as to the policy of abandoning the purpose to keep the oil in the ground which has, except for a feeble voice lately raised in the House, had no defender in either body. The public, however, so far as the press indicated, remained apathetic.

In the interim stories had reached me, rumors rather, about some significant land deal in New Mexico, — sometimes it was Fall who purchased for Sinclair, again Sinclair who purchased for Fall. They were vague in character, and diligent inquiry revealed no details. The statement above as to the press is too general. A few newspapers early sensed the importance of the revelations, notably the St. Louis "Post-Despatch," the Omaha "World Herald," the Raleigh "News and Observer," and the Washington "Daily News," a Scripps publication. From the Honorable W. B. Colver, editor of the last named, I learned that the Denver "Post," which virulently denounced the lease at the outset and then strangely and suddenly quit, had in the summer of 1922 sent a man to New Mexico to investigate the land deal and that he had made a report which, for some reason, the "Post" had omitted to publish. Rumors of why the "Post" had changed its policy fed the suspicion with which I viewed the transaction.

Through Colver and his Denver connections I learned that the reporter was friendly but fearful and that his report, still available, was interesting. I had no funds at my command to bring him to Washington. I had no investigator at my service to interview him or any one. I went before the Committee and asked for a subpoena to require his attendance. Grudgingly authority for its issuance was awarded. He came with his report and gave the names and addresses of witnesses in New Mexico who could tell of Fall's sudden rise from financial embarrassment, if not impecuniosity, to comparative affluence. He brought certified copies of the records showing the acquisition by Fall of the Harris ranch, of his delinquencies in the matter of his local taxes extending over a period of ten years, and of his liquidation of them in the summer of 1922, and of the shipment of blooded stock from Sinclair's farm in New Jersey to Fall's ranch in New Mexico.

I then dismissed him and secured subpoenas for the New Mexico witness, who told the story of Fall's having paid $91,500 for the ranch mentioned, — the initial payment of $10,000 having been made in bills taken from a black tin box, — of his subsequent purchase of other lands costing $33,000 more, of the installation of a hydro-electric plant at a cost of from $40,000 to $50,000, and of other expenditures in the aggregate approximating $200,000. I did not enter into that field of inquiry without misgivings. Seeking advice from a friendly associate on the Committee, I was assured that some plausible story would be told and the effort come to naught. I determined, however, that the duty of the Committee being to investigate, the witnesses should be called, whatever might be the outcome. The significance of their testimony, synchronizing in its details so strangely with Sinclair's visit in his private car to Fall's ranch in the latter part of 1921, an added circumstance of a suspicious character, could not be overlooked and gave rise to obvious consternation among the friends of Fall on the Committee who were, however, reassured by a message from him to the effect that his son-in-law, who was entirely conversant with his business affairs, would come on to explain all.

By this time there was attracted to the committee room an increasing number of representatives of the press, but though the daily reports of the proceedings were reasonably complete, the editorial force seemed oblivious of what was going on. It was at about that stage of the inquiry that I sought through influential friends to arouse the interest of some of the metropolitan papers which, for one reason or another, might be expected to aid, for I realized that many might be prompted to help should the issue be agitated who would otherwise remain silent. If they made any effort it was fruitless. Doheny coming upon the stand about that time denounced as an "outrage" the bringing of witnesses from New Mexico to besmirch the character of so upright a public official as Albert B. Fall. More recent denunciatory comment on the investigators does not specify Fall or any other particular individual, for that matter. But at that time I was a muckraker, vilifying worthy public servants.

Still it was up to Fall to tell where the money came from. His son-in-law did not appear according to promise. Fall did not. A statement made by him to the press gave the assurance that a full explanation would be made. Later it was reported in a vague way that he was ill, — now in Chicago, now in New York. Reporters were unable to locate him, for they were now on the job. In fact he came to Chicago, went from there to New York, thence to Atlantic City, and to Washington where he had an interview with Senators Smoot and Lenroot, members of the Committee, and with Will Hays, late Chairman of the Republican National Committee, to whom he told, as he did in a letter to the Committee on December 27, 1923, that he had borrowed $100,000 with which to purchase the Harris Ranch, from Edward B. McLean, owner and editor of the Washington "Post," then at Palm Beach, Florida, whither Fall speedily betook himself as McLean's guest.

The same volubility which characterized his testimony was in evidence in his written communication to the Committee.

It bore intrinsic evidence of being of doubtful veracity. A month had gone by since the damaging evidence had been heard. An honest man would have hastened to take the stand to refute the inferences to which it naturally gave rise and the doubts that it must inevitably have raised. Had such a man been desperately ill he would have told the story on the stand and not sought refuge from cross-examination by sending a letter from his hotel in the city in which the committee was sitting. Moreover, the knowing ones smiled incredulously at the idea of Ned McLean's having such a sum of money at hand to loan, though rich in property, or of his loaning it if he had it.

Forthwith that gentleman began to exhibit a feverish anxiety lest he be called as a witness, singularly divining what was coming. He communicated by wire with the Committee; he sent lawyers to represent to it and to me that he was ill, that his wife was ill; that it would be dangerous for him to tempt the rigorous climate of Washington at that season of the year; that he had loaned $100,000 to Fall in November or December, 1922; that he knew nothing about the facts otherwise; that he would make a written statement under oath if the Committee desired him to attest to the truth of a statement he would send. He begged not to be called to Washington. I was insistent that he appear; other members of the Committee were disposed to be accommodating, and on a record vote on which I and my supporters were outnumbered, it was agreed to take from him a statement and hold in abeyance until it was received his plea to be excused.

In the discussion Senator Smoot suggested that I go to Palm Beach and take his testimony. That seemed to me impracticable in view of the demands upon my time, but leave was given to me to submit interrogatories to be answered in connection with his statement. But on attempting to draft such I became convinced that the effort to get the truth by that method would be unavailing and I signified to the Committee my willingness to go to Palm Beach. The proper authority to take his testimony was given and on the 11th of January he confronted me at "The Breakers."

I made the trip in the expectation that he would say that he had made the loan, intending to interrogate him as to the source from which the money was derived. I proposed to trace it to its source, either to his own private funds, kept in his own private account, or to some account earmarked in a manner that would permit following it to some other origin. I suspected that in some way it came from Sinclair and that I could follow it through various banking transactions to that source. It had not occurred to me that it might have come from Doheny, though it had been disclosed, — a fact of which Fall omitted to make any mention when on the stand, — that the whole of Naval Reserve No. 1 in California, 32,000 acres in area, estimated to contain 250,000,000 barrels of oil, had been on December 11, 1922, leased to Doheny, who afterwards told us that he too expected to make $100,000,000 out of his lease secured from Fall in the same secret manner as had characterized the Sinclair deal.

I was dumbfounded when McLean, evidently appreciating that he would be required to tell the bank upon which he drew to make the loan to Fall, should he adhere to his earlier story, frankly admitted that he never did loan the money to Fall adding that he gave Fall his checks for that sum which were returned a few days later and destroyed without being cashed, the recipient asserting that he had arranged to secure the necessary elsewhere.

Now the affair could no longer be kept off the front page. Leading news gatherers sent representatives to Palm Beach to report the proceedings there; but the country was not fully aroused until on January 21 the Roosevelts went on the stand to relate their lurid story, and the climax was reached when on January 24 Doheny voluntarily appeared to tell that on November 30, 1921, he had loaned $100,000 to Fall without security, moved by old friendship and commiseration for his business misfortunes, negotiations between them then pending eventuating in the contract awarded to Doheny on April 25, following, through which he secured, without competition, a contract giving him a preference right to a lease of a large part of Naval Reserve No. 1, to be followed by the lease of the whole of it, as above recited.

Followed the appearance of Fall, forced by the Committee to come before it, after pleading inability on account of illness, to take refuge under his constitutional immunity, a broken man, the cynosure of the morbidly curious that crowded all approaches to the committee room and packed it to suffocation, vindicating the wisdom of the patriarch who proclaimed centuries ago that the way of the transgressor is hard.

U.S. Congress, Senate. 68th Cong., 1st Sess. Committee on Public Lands and Surveys. Leases upon Naval Oil Reserves. [*Testimony of Edward L. Doheny.*] *Hearings, Part 7, pp. 1939–40. February 1, 1924*

The CHAIRMAN. Until yesterday. Now, have you employed any other ex-Cabinet officers?

Mr. DOHENY. Yes, sir.

The CHAIRMAN. Who?

Mr. DOHENY. At the time when our properties were greatly menaced in Mexico by the hostile attitude of the Mexican Government I employed ex-Secretary McAdoo. . . .

The CHAIRMAN. Now, very well, go on with Mr. McAdoo.

Mr. DOHENY. I employed Mr. McAdoo because of his —

The CHAIRMAN. One moment. When was your employment of Mr. McAdoo.

Mr. DOHENY. I think it was — I am not certain about dates. It might have been a year after he left the Cabinet. He was a member of the firm of McAdoo, Cotton & Franklin, and I employed the firm — Mr. McAdoo was a member of that firm — to represent us in Washington in connection with Mexican matters.

The CHAIRMAN. In Washington?

Mr. DOHENY. Yes, sir.

The CHAIRMAN. Can you tell us the year? Well, that was about a year after, you said?

Mr. DOHENY. Well, that was about a year after he resigned from the Cabinet.

The CHAIRMAN. Could you furnish to the committee the exact date of that employment?

Mr. DOHENY. I think I have got it on our books. Yes, sir, I am quite sure it is on our books.

The CHAIRMAN. And how long did Mr. McAdoo continue to represent you?

Mr. DOHENY. Mr. McAdoo continued to represent us in that regard until the Mexican situation was practically completed. That is, until the administration changed.

The CHAIRMAN. That is, he continued to represent you so long as Mr. Wilson's administration remained?

Mr. DOHENY. So long as he was President, yes sir. And after that he didn't represent us in Washington any longer, except that he represented us in Mexico. And he made a trip to Mexico in connection with our affairs, the Palomas Land & Cattle Co.

The CHAIRMAN. And does he still represent you?

Mr. DOHENY. And he still represents us.

The CHAIRMAN. He still represents you?

Mr. DOHENY. Yes, sir.

The CHAIRMAN. Were his services for you during the last administration compensated for?

Mr. DOHENY. Yes, sir.

The CHAIRMAN. Will you tell the committee how much you paid Mr. McAdoo?

Mr. DOHENY. All told I think about $250,000.

The CHAIRMAN. $250,000?

Mr. DOHENY. I think so, all told.

The CHAIRMAN. I would be glad if you could furnish us the facts with reference to the time; that is, how long after his resignation as Secretary of the Treasury?

Mr. DOHENY. Well, I will furnish you that. There is no difficulty about getting those facts, Senator Lenroot.

WALTER LIPPMANN,
CHESTER ROWELL, AND HERBERT CROLY
Why I Shall Vote for   I. Davis; II. Coolidge; III. La Follette, *The New Republic, XL, October 29, 1924, pp. 218–223*

I. DAVIS

I shall vote for Mr. Davis because he is the only man who can be elected in place of Mr. Coolidge, and I do not wish directly or indirectly to give the present administration another term of power. I shall vote for Mr. Davis because it seems to me highly important that the next President should be willing to coöperate with Europe in organizing the peace of the world. I shall vote for him because it seems to me important that the next President should be neither bewildered, antipathetic nor obtuse in the face of the present sectional and class divisions. I shall vote for him because I believe that in this post-war world of fierce nationalisms his strong Jeffersonian bias against the concentration and exaggeration of government is more genuinely liberal than much that goes by the name of liberalism.

In short, I think it more important to vote so as to determine the character of the administration in the next four years than to vote for a new party system which may or may not be established in 1928 or in 1932. Perhaps the immediate consequences would not seem so much more real to me if I saw in the La Follette movement the materials and the ideals of a great liberalizing effort.

First, the practical politics of the La Follette movement. Here in the East its supporters, the New Republic among them, are arguing that the new party is to destroy and supplant the Democratic party as the opposition to conservative Republicanism. This seems to me impossible. The Democratic party is more or less indestructible because of the solid South. A party which enters every campaign with roughly half the electoral votes is not in my opinion going to disappear. It seems extremely unlikely that La Follette will break the solid South, and almost as unlikely that the Southern Democrats will coalesce, as the New Republic has suggested, with the Eastern Republicans. If the Democratic party survives, and if the Republican party survives, there is not under the presidential system of government any permanent future for a third party. I believe the La Follette movement is almost certain to be re-absorbed into the two old parties. It might dominate one of them for a time, as Bryan dominated the Democratic party with one interval from 1896 to 1912. But in the sense that it will make a new party system, intellectually distinct, emotionally honest, logical, clear cut and free of cant, I do not believe in the promises made in its name.

I think the exponents of the new party have never really understood the federal character of the American party system, have never understood that we have in fact no national parties, but only national coalitions of state parties, and that as long as the President is not directly elected by a plurality of voters, the vitality of the party will remain in the state organizations. These state parties are independent bodies which come together every four years, as La Follette's Wisconsin and Lodge's Massachusetts used to come together. The national conventions set out to unite the state organizations on the basis of formulae which won't seriously divide them, and under the leadership of candidates who are popular in the dominant groups of states and acceptable to the others.

I shall not undertake here to argue whether this system is as absurd as it sounds, except to note in passing that it is the only political system we know under which a continental state has

combined a strong central government with wide home rule.
The British system of government is no analogy whatsoever,
and even if it were, its comparative failure to deal successfully
with Ireland and Ulster should be set beside the American success with half a dozen potential Irelands and Ulsters. In fact,
I believe that the discerning historian will recognize more
clearly than we can or perhaps need to do, that the success of
federalism in America has depended largely upon the sectional
accommodations achieved through our flexible and unprincipled
two-party system.

But whether or not the fundamental virtues of that system
outweigh its obvious stupidities, its frequent venality and its
intellectual sterility, it is so deeply imbedded in our social system that it will, I think, upset the plans of Mr. La Follette's
supporters. I should feel less certain of this if it were not already apparent that the La Follette movement is yielding to
the same conditions. It too is a coalition of local organizations,
and this early in its career, it exhibits all the symptoms of that
same equivocation which the unifying of diverse elements requires. On foreign policy, on the question of whether to break
up monopoly or socialize it, on immigration, on prohibition,
even on the Supreme Court, the La Follette movement speaks
with an uncertain voice or none at all. Why is that so? The
New Republic, as I understand it, has argued that the La Follette movement was a gathering of the disfranchised and dis-
satisfied, and that when they were gathered they would unite
on a coherent platform. I am skeptical about this explanation.
For I think Mr. La Follette was shrewd enough to know that
his hope of uniting his followers lay in avoiding the issues that
divide them. He acted as every political leader does and for
the same reasons and under the same compulsions. And when I
see the New Republic making a virtue of Progressive ambiguities while it expends its scorn on Democratic and Republican
ambiguities, I smell the old familiar business of rationalizing
your partisanship.

I am prepared to admit, of course, that I am misreading the political situation and that in some way a significant and profound realignment of parties will result. But this possibility seems to me too remote and doubtful to overcome the feeling that it is very important not to give this administration four more years of power. I might vote for La Follette, nevertheless, if I felt that he was the exponent of a genuine liberal and progressive movement. For it might be worth while to ignore the character of the next administration for the sake of the educative effect of the La Follette movement.

But in many ways, and even though I warmly respect Mr. La Follette, I do not like the main drift of his preaching. His political program is almost violently nationalistic and centralizing; that seems to me reactionary and illiberal. His policy in respect to large corporations seems to me an illogical mixture of the individualism of 1890, as expressed in the Sherman Act, and pre-war Socialism. His foreign policy seems to date about 1919, and to ignore all that has happened in Europe since the Treaty of Versailles was first published. The net effect of what he has to say about Europe is to combine American irresponsibility and isolation with provocative statements about the policies of France and England.

I feel that if I am to cast my vote for a candidate who cannot be elected, and by that vote to help elect the man I think ought not to be elected, then at least I ought to be able to vote for a man who is bravely and lucidly expounding what seems to me a liberal program. Mr. La Follette does not offer me that compensation. I shall therefore vote for Mr. Davis because in foreign policy and in his attitude toward the sphere of government he seems to me to be on the right track, more nearly on the right track than either of the two other candidates. I shall vote for him, not only believing that he is headed in the right direction, but that in personal character and in experience of the post-war world he is the best equipped man. And if the movement for a new party system has the vitality claimed for it, it will, I think, be helped rather than obstructed by the presence in the White House of a man able to understand it, and resourceful enough to put it on its mettle.

WALTER LIPPMANN.

II. COOLIDGE

As a Progressive — of that perhaps obsolescent sort that still believes in democracy — I have decided to support Coolidge. Not, of course, that I agree with him in everything, or that I accept unreservedly the Republicanism of the moment; but because, on the realities of the case, this seems to me the most practical way now available to make one citizen's vote and influence effective for democracy.

Recent inquiry develops that nearly all those who were most conspicuous in the Roosevelt movement of 1912 are now for Coolidge and that in their opinion this is also the position of the main body of the Progressive voters of that time. Of the few who are not for Coolidge, as many are for Davis as for La Follette. Whether this means that these people are not now Progressives, or that the newest La Follettism which seeks to appropriate the name is something else than Progressive, may be left to those who enjoy quibbling over definitions. At any rate, this, the largest concrete group that ever called itself "Progressive" does not concede the title to La Follette, and anyone who goes with them to Coolidge will not find himself lost in reactionary company. I can of course only speak for myself, but I am confident that the views I am here expressing are fairly typical of those of millions of others of this group who have reached the same conclusion.

"A condition, not a theory, confronts us." What this campaign will determine practically is not which candidate is elected, but whether there is an election. Davis cannot be elected. Coolidge cannot be elected by a scratch. He must have a substantial margin over Davis or he will have none over all. La Follette is not even running to be elected. He is running to prevent election. Either Coolidge will be elected by the people or we shall have a President not elected by the people. That might be no objection if, like most extreme radicals and reactionaries, one did not believe in democracy. But it happens I do. I cling even to its forms, because without them I fear for the substance. The mere mechanism of popular government — even if, this year, it seemed nothing more — is a tool tremendously worth holding intact for continued use. Those who are now trying to break it down would not think it worth their while unless they hoped also to block it next time, and more times. If that must happen I am willing, after it is done, to help build something hopeful on the wreckage. I am not willing to be a party to the wrecking.

Neither can I be indifferent to the practical outcome. I do not want Charles W. Bryan to be President. Of the six candidates for President and Vice-President, he is the only one who falls preposterously short of what we have come to consider the presidential measure. Did you ever read the "Commoner" while he was running it, with "W. J." as absentee contributor? If not, spare yourself the shock! He is touted as the one "Progressive" in the major party field. Emotionally, he doubtless is progressive. But if mere "one hundred percent for the people" sentiment were all, Andy Gump would be the ideal candidate. Governor Bryan's Nebraska policies have been both progressive and reactionary, with no indication that he knew which was which. Administratively he is a putterer, who would be lost in a great executive place. We may accept constructive conservatism as one of the periodic phases in the rhythm of democracy — but not that caliber of futile pseudo-progressivism.

Or, if we look beyond this election to the future, the case is even stronger. The personal candidacy of Senator La Follette cannot in the course of nature be repeated. Unless something capable of impersonal survival can come of it, his movement ends in a mere negative protest this year. That something could only be a third party avowedly founded on class. Now, I may be archaic, palaeocrystic, obsolete, Byzantine, mid-Victorian, and all the other back-number epithets in the thesaurus, but I am not ready to accept class as the basis of political division in America. If the economic determinists are correct, it is coming anyway — but not with my help! I concede the many absurdities in the established parties. Some of us tried twelve years ago to make them contemporaneous and failed. Now the advanced intelligentsia think that we, too, have ceased to be contemporaneous. But until something better can be had — and a group system of class parties would be something much worse — even these "atavistic" parties do serve a useful purpose. They may have been bulldozed at times by class blocs — business, farm, soldier and labor — but they are not class parties. By their appeal for support from all classes and sections they are a potent factor of national unity. And they are mechanically capable of operating our national electoral apparatus — something physically impossible under the class bloc system. For these services, in the hope that they may grow also to better ones, much may be forgiven them.

Whatever may be the alignment of the future, the Republican party will be either one of the major parties or the parent of one. Leaving it for the future to determine whether, when it thus finds its place, I shall go with it or against it, I think I am of more present use in helping to hold it intact than I would be in joining with those who, in disintegrating it, would disrupt the whole party system.

If we are headed toward class group parties, it is not toward one or three, but many. The mere fact that Senator La Follette did not dare form a party this time, but merely invited the personal support of discordant groups who agreed in nothing else, illustrates the centrifugal tendency. As soon as you get more than two significant parties, you either go back to two or you get more than three. Whatever may happen in England, no class party in America is going to reduce the rest of the people to another class party, and so make a two party system out of that. It will either fizzle, or tend to a multi-party system. I prefer to help it fizzle. I have seen too much of the undemocratic operation of the multi-party system in Europe to be willing to do anything to help introduce it in America. It does work somehow in Europe, even if badly. Here, it would not work at all. We could not even elect a President, organize Congress, or legislate under it, except by making over our whole structure of government. If we ever do that, it should be contructively, to make government more efficient and not merely defensively, to keep it from being stopped.

A platform may not be much reason for supporting a party, but it sometimes contains reasons for opposing it. I am therefore not so much impressed with the things in the La Follette platform and in his historic personal policies with which I agree, as I am repelled by those which I now find dangerous.

La Follette's whole isolationist position, internationally, I find reactionary to the last degree. In all European Parliaments, the Nationalist Isolationists sit on the extremest Right, with Ludendorff or Léon Daudet. I think that is where they belong here. The one exception which he has dragged into his platform is done for pure demagogy, to catch the hyphenate German vote. If what La Follette were really interested in were the legitimate revision of the Treaty of Versailles, he would not have proposed the only method of attack which would guarantee failure.

And of course I do not agree with his scheme to abolish the Constitution, by making Congress the final judge of the constitutionality of its own acts. Minorities — particularly the very class, racial and religious minorities which La Follette is now trying to lump together — are precisely the last Americans who should be willing to surrender the constitutional safeguards. The remedy for the faults of our courts does not lie in that direction. If we must make over our government, let us begin with Congress where it works worst, and not with the courts, which, with all their faults, have protected democracy oftener than privilege. A study, not of adversely selected cases, but of cases generally, will demonstrate this emphatically as to the federal courts. There are better remedies than this, for the cases where this is not true. The proposal to make federal courts elective for short terms is not progressive, but reactionary.

With these reasons for not supporting La Follette, with his assumption of first right to progressive support, the question lies between Davis and Coolidge. I admire Davis personally very much, and I agree with some of his policies even better than with Coolidge's. Any objection that he is a "conservative" might also lie against Coolidge. If it were a mere choice of individuals, I should not worry. Progressives might have to do some impatient marking time under either of them, but the country would be safe, and its course, even if cautious, would be forward.

But in the first place we can not get Davis. In the states which will decide the election, a vote for Davis, like a vote for La Follette, is a vote for no election. And in the second place, for reasons too long to analyze here, I see no constructive prospect in the hodge-podge which is now the Democratic party. If it or some other party is needed as the opposition, I do not care whether it is it or some other. I have no interest in contributing to its evolution or devolution. I do feel that interest in the Republican party.

And I share the national confidence in Calvin Coolidge. Deride the "Coolidge myth" all you like, such traditions do not grow out of nothing. President Coolidge has been under test. To have come through the greatest storm of scandal that has stirred our generation, not merely personally untouched, but with his vessel unwrecked, is a test of results that is not vitiated by any temperamental criticism that he should have been more emotionally dramatic about it. I long ago learned that each person must do things his own way. If it is a good way, and does the work, it is nothing against it that it is not my way. He has shown courage, judgment, intelligence and leadership, in his relations with the people. I am willing to hope that he will be better-armed next time in his relations with Congress. And — one count on the progressive side — I have confidence in his personal independence of reactionary influence. The "Old Guard" may be for him, but he is not for them.

If I were making a candidate and a party to order, I would doubtless propose some amendments to President Coolidge, and many more to the present régime of the Republican party. But upon the whole concrete situation, at a time when the menace to democracy is even more immediate from destructive radicalism and disruptive multi-partyism than from capitalized privilege, and seeing in President Coolidge a force that is at least constructive, and is as near progressive as is now available if we also demand balance and intelligence, I have no hesitation in making my choice.

And I believe that this expresses a view typical of at least a very large part of that group who were once called "Progressives" and who still believe that there is vitality in the Lincoln and Roosevelt ideal of unclassified Americanism.

CHESTER H. ROWELL.

III. LA FOLLETTE

The welfare of the American people demands in my opinion the accomplishment by peaceful agitation under the forms of law of certain radical changes in the structure and functions of their national economy and government. The processes whereby wealth is produced, distributed and protected tend in many respects to breed extravagant, shiftless, torpid, intolerant, unenlightened, self-satisfied and undeveloped American citizens. Yet these processes are deeply rooted in the social and economic soil. They are so deeply rooted that ardent, impatient and turbulent spirits have despaired of uprooting them save by some act of destructive violence comparable to the French or the Russian Revolutions. But there is an alternative way which is more suitable, more exhilarating and more congenial to humane ideals. It is, of course, the way of educating a majority of the people to understand the need of radical reconstruction, to discriminate those reforms which are desirable and possible from those which are not, and to participate themselves in the work of renewal. I shall vote for Senator La Follette because in my opinion his election will contribute more substantially than that of his competitors to the needed social and political education of the American people.

Cherishing as I do the vision of a moral and social order which will interpose fewer obstacles between human beings and their fulfillment, I obviously cannot vote for President Coolidge. He is the spokesman of those classes which are satisfied with the effect of the existing system upon the moral quality of the average American. His advocacy is sincere and whole-hearted. The human race will be fortunate, indeed, if its presumably more enlightened leaders of the future can evolve or devise economic or social institutions which will work as satisfactorily as in Mr. Coolidge's opinion our present institutions work. Or to put it in franker language the President's complacency about the America of today is almost incredible in its fatuous ignorance and in its essential absurdity. Historians will smile when they turn over the records and discover that in the first quarter of the 20th century people who called themselves progressives proclaimed reasons ostensibly associated with progressivism for keeping in the presidential chair a man who believed that the America of that day was by way of being Utopian in its successful realization of the loftiest ideals.

President Coolidge's self-righteous complacency is only the reflection of the moral outlook of his prosperous and successful fellow countrymen. The immediate weakness of American capitalism does not consist so much in its abuses. These abuses are not as yet intolerable and against them its defenders can offset considerable and indispensable services. It consists in the tendency of its beneficiaries deliberately to cultivate a state of mind which, if it continues to prevail, will make it extremely difficult if not impossible, to remedy these abuses in an orderly and thorough manner. The Republicans insist upon lumping

together the whole existing economic system with its successful and unsuccessful, admirable and mischievous practices and
fabrics into one indivisible whole and to condemn all people
who wish radically to modify it as the enemies, and usually as
malicious enemies, of American popular welfare. American
business men and their professional spokesmen combine blindness to abuses with resistance to reform and reprobation of
reformers. They are tender to the Lorimers, Newberries,
Daugherties and Sinclairs. They are fierce against the La
Follettes. It is this attitude, suggestive as it is of a too close
association between profits and abuses, which has produced the
equally aggressive conscious resistance of the La Follette radicalism. Responsible business men have become intensely class-
conscious themselves, and they have, consequently, created
and justified the existence of an opposing class-consciousness
among the people who suffer from their selfishness and obscur-
antism.

The Republicans of the Dawes type who dominate organized
business in the United States will, if they have their way, ruin
by their violence and their pigheadedness precious but fallible
institutions. They will resist as socially subversive the inevitable
attempt to disentangle the ill-adjusted functions in the national
economy from those which are working comparatively well,
and they will, consequently, do their best to involve the latter
in the radical revision which must eventually overtake the former. It is, of course, of vital importance that they should not
succeed. The possibility of modifying in an orderly and edi-
fying way those institutions and practices which are most
inimical to the better fulfillment of human life in America
depends primarily on the willingness and the ability of our
business and political rulers to discriminate between those institutions and industries which are functioning well and those
which are functioning ill. If the present rulers are neither willing nor able to undertake the job, other more flexible and capable rulers with a different economic and social outlook will

have to be substituted for them. The period of transition will be anxious and chaotic, but the responsibility for this uncertainty belongs to those who profit from the failures and weaknesses of the existing national economy and enshrine their profits in the ark of the Constitution.

II

Davis and La Follette are agreed in repudiating the colossal complacency of Coolidge and the stupid violence of men like Dawes. They are agreed in proclaiming that an economic and political system does and should survive by virtue of some measure of flexibility rather than by structural rigidity and functional blindness. But their differences are more considerable and more significant than their agreements. The changes which Mr. Davis would immediately prepare to bring about are few and superficial. They do not touch the existing distribution of political and economic power. For Mr. Davis a progressive program is a group of reforms which the Democratic party, whose active and responsible leaders are the conservative lawyers, business men and professional politicians of their own neighborhoods, is fully capable of realizing. La Follette's program, on the other hand, is the reflection and expression of the salient interests of the members of those classes which the existing system deprives of a sufficient opportunity for liberating activity. Such a program involves necessarily the participation of these comparatively disfranchised classes in carrying it out, and, consequently, in the creation of new agencies of political and economic power for whose operation they will become at least partly responsible.

The Democratic apologists are as definitely, if not as violently, opposed to this demand for independent political power on the part of farmer-labor groups as are the Republicans. They ask the wage-earner or the farmer to trust his economic welfare to a party organization and leaders belonging to a class whose members derive their living chiefly from salaries, interest, rent and profits and whose ideas reflect their activities.

They denounce the attempt to build up a political party composed primarily of the classes who live by work as an attack upon the moral unity of American national life. But if the moral unity of the American nation is endangered, the threat comes from those people, who, under the cover of vested interests, partly obsolete institutions and popular inertia are appropriating too large a share of the power and rewards of American life, and who refuse either to share the power or to criticize its exercise. The insurgents discern and propose to thwart the existing tendency to convert the American Commonwealth into a complacent industrialized plutocracy. They do not trust either of the major parties to perform the job because the leaders of both belong to the classes whose conduct, outlook and personal welfare are determined by profitable abuses. No matter how well-intentioned they be, they are bound, as Mr. Davis does, to identify progressivism with a little mild squeamishness about such matters as child labor and the denial to organized labor of the right of collective bargaining. Progressivism of this kind is not intended and will not help to prepare the way for an improved distribution of economic and political power. Its tendency and purpose are to prevent such a new distribution from taking place.

III

The class which has profited from the rapid industrial expansion of this country will never yield its anti-social privileges or modify its mechanism of superiority except as the result of sharp, persistent and implacable pressure. There is no political force in the community which can or will exert the needed pressure except the several large economic groups, which at present are not allowed to count as much as their services and responsibilities entitle them to count in the organization and conduct of American government and industry. The only way in which these groups can acquire the edge and the energy to challenge the domination of their economic and political superiors is to cultivate an aggressive consciousness of their group

activities and interests — to become much more keenly and res-
olutely aware than they now are of their inferior status and the
desirability of obtaining promotion by their own political and
economic efforts. Increased awareness of their existing status
is the preliminary stage of a necessary educational preparation
for the better future exercise of more responsibility and power.

So far, then, from deploring or fearing the organization of a
farmer-labor party, I believe it to be the fitting instrument of
the orderly but sufficiently thorough-going readjustment of
American political and economic life. My chief misgiving about
my vote and other votes for La Follette is that they may not
avail to bring such a party into existence. That it will come
eventually I fully believe, but, as art is long and time is short,
it needs to come soon. Many of Senator La Follette's present
supporters do not realize how indispensable the conscious political and other self-assertion of economic groups is to the education of the American people and the exercise of improved
control over their lives. The larger part of the support which
the Senator will obtain at the coming election will be composed
in part of conscious or semi-conscious workers, but he will obtain millions of votes which will express merely a mechanical
protest against Democracy and Republicanism or some form of
hyphenated discontent. American progressivism in its political
expression is still far from being a coherent, articulate and self-
conscious demonstration. Although it may soon win the support of a sufficient fraction of the American people to elect
a president, it is only beginning to educate a personnel which
in the event of victory could serve as the adequate human instrument of its purposes.

Hence I cannot attach as much importance as do some of
his other supporters to the excellence of Mr. La Follette's
achievements in Wisconsin as the chief reason for preferring
him. That record surely proves him to be a capable legislator
and administrator, but these evidences of his competence in
the past do not, I think, shed much light on his ability to

accomplish the task of radical reconstruction to which the Progressives are pledged in national politics. The old Wisconsin program is allied to the present program of the Progressives, but it was a program of middle-class legislative reform, such as one of the existing parties could conceivably frame and carry out; and it did not need to enlist to the same extent, as does the more radical program of today, the understanding and the participation of the members of those classes which it is supposed to benefit. The re-organization of American railroads, finance, industry and agriculture in the interest of improved production, diminished waste and of increased participation in the control and conduct of economic processes by the workers is a very different matter from the task which Mr. La Follette faced in Wisconsin. I know of no specific program which looks adequate for accomplishing the desired results. I know of no trustworthy social experience and formulated knowledege out of which the leaders of a progressive party could devise such a program. I know of no class of workers who are sufficiently trained in the exercise of political and economic power to operate the improved mechanism, if it could be devised. A progressive agitation which assumes that these instruments already exist and are available for use in the event of success at the polls is suffering from a serious and perhaps a dangerous delusion.

Yet if this ignorance and incompetence provided a sound reason for refusing to support La Follette, there would be no hope for future reconstruction. The knowledge which is necessary for the framing of an adequate program, and the improved popular education which is necessary to carry it out, can be obtained only by experimental essays undertaken with the help of the existing available stock of knowledge and method. A progressive bloc composed of the members of those classes which need and consciously seek more active and responsible participation in government and economic production is the only agency which will have the courage and the

insight to make sufficiently thorough-going and significant experiments. These experiments cannot in the beginning be protected against miscarriage. The knowledge does not exist which
would justify experts who might also be progressive in recom-
mending a program which could be guaranteed as relevant and
adequate. Thorough-going progressives must be ready to act
on the supposition that human beings are capable of an amount
and a quality of liberation for which the society of today
neither affords the opportunity nor supplies trustworthy instruments. If no sufficient number of people will act as if the
vision of increasing human liberation in this world were true,
the human mind will never find out how true it may be. . . .

HERBERT CROLY.

ARTHUR KROCK
The Damn Fool Democrats, *The American Mercury, IV, March
1925, pp. 257–262*

FROM the traditional Democratic viewpoint, the Madison
Square Garden convention of last Summer was the most enjoyable ever held. That means two other things. One, to have
been enjoyable it must have been sanguinary. Two, having
been sanguinary, and therefore enjoyable, it was, in the Democratic sense, highly successful.

It is true, of course, that the party lost the ensuing election,
lost it by the largest popular and Electoral College majorities
in the record. It is true also that the Republicans will retain
all the Federal offices and the salaries appertaining thereto for
four long years. But the fact remains unchanged: there never
was so successful a convention, from the Democratic viewpoint,
as the snarling, cursing, tedious, tenuous, suicidal, homicidal
rough-house in New York City last July.

For, while the fight may have cost many Democrats regular
meals, all Democrats would rather fight than eat. And while a
fight with the Republicans has a certain element of appeal, it

involves the adoption of a definite punctilio, and that spoils the fun for a true Democrat. To be required to temper his speech, to convey the manifestly impossible admission that a Republican may have blood, brains, piety and worth in the same ratio as a Democrat — these are the responsibilities of an open fight before the electorate which bore with inexpressible ennui the true disciple of Jefferson and Jackson. It is only a combat with other Democrats that a thorough Jacksonian really enjoys. To that he advances at the double, carrying every lethal weapon in his arsenal. Parents, brothers, cousins: let any of these bar his path as, with nervous fingers, he rushes toward the jugular of another Democrat, and patricide and fratricide become mere misdemeanors. . . .

The constituent parts of a Democratic convention are always the same. From the South come the Scotch-Irish. From the East and Middle West come the Irish of the lakes and fells. No sooner do they meet than a Cockran is cracking the poll of a Bryan, and the McAdoos and the Brennans are at it, tooth and nail. The few Sassenachs, Germans, Jews and Latins who make up the rest of the roster mill timidly and uneasily about the battlefield. Gradually they become Republicans. If you don't like a fight for the pure Celtic lilt of it, you have no real place in the Democratic party.

After the factions are exhausted physically, and have exploded enough political dynamite under everybody put in nomination to leave only remnants out of which to make candidates, the tattered standard is thrust into the broken hands of a punch-drunk politician and he is pushed out into the lists where the unmaimed Republican candidate awaits him. If by chance he wins, he instantly becomes uninteresting to his partisans, for it is only adversity that fires the Democratic spirit. And his administration is soon split in as many directions as could be indicated by a thistledown weathercock in a typhoon. If he loses, those who nominated him surround him with the halo of martyrdom and swear they will never permit the standard to be wrested from his hand. It was treachery that did it, they cry; and treachery shall never be met with compromise.

So at the very next convention the martyr is the centre of another battle. And having the appeal of sentiment on his side, he is nominated again. The oftener he loses, and the more bitterly he takes his defeat, the dearer he becomes to those who are responsible for him. For when Democrats fasten upon a really consistent loser they cannot bear to part with him. All the springs of poetry well up within their breasts. His presence reminds everybody of beautiful fights in the past and is a living promise of more. Hence three nominations for William Jennings Bryan. Hence the undying McAdoo. Both have the perfume of defeat upon them. Both are bad and frequent losers. Both mean a terrific row in any convention where they are active. Nothing else could so appeal to the Democratic spirit....

Probably the Democratic party in July, 1924, had no real chance to defeat President Coolidge. But the Democratic party believed otherwise. It had been out of Federal office for four years. The by-elections of 1922 had shown a receding Republican tide. There was every political reason why the Madison Square Garden convention should have been the scene of reasonable compromise between the factions. Republicans, in similar case, would have smoothed out everything in two days of pre-convention conference.

But that wouldn't have been poetry. That wouldn't have been battle. That wouldn't have been Democratic. A puling convention without Bryan baiting Tammany, without the West embattled against the East — what follower of Jackson worthy of his heritage would have weighed victory and office against the cherished diversions of his fathers? So the Scotch-Irish and the regular Irish rushed at each other again amid a bashing of heads and breast-bones and a crunching of legs and arms which continued until everybody lay groaning happily on the battle-field. And as the delegates crawled away, the knowledge that they had no chance to defeat the Republicans did not distress them. The Smith boys whispered that they had made the hellions of McAdoo holler enough, and the McAdoo boys anointed their wounds with the glorious balm of certain party defeat. The true spirit of democracy had triumphed; on the shrine lay the smoking sacrifices; all was well. And unless the party undergoes a deterioration of spirit between now and 1928 the beautiful scrap will then be fought all over again.

That cat-calls differ according to the caprice of the period. In 1896 one yelled "silver" and the other "gold." In 1920 one cried "wet" and the other "dry." In 1924 one bawled "Klan" and the other "Papist." But the method and the result are always the same. On the rare occasions when languor produces compromise, no Democrat enjoys himself. The convention of 1904, save for the brief flurry of the Parker gold telegram to Sheehan, was as dull as a Standard Oil board meeting. The convention of 1916, where there was nothing to do but renominate Woodrow Wilson, made the delegates sigh for the shambles at Baltimore. To a Republican, conventions like these are the light of his eyes and the breath of his nostrils. They mean victory, jobs, power, high tariff bills, White House receptions, Gridiron dinners, peace. To a Democrat they are ghastly because he cannot smell the warm odor of his party's life blood. . . .

The Republicans love fraternal peace and a winner. The Democrats love internecine war and a loser. The Republicans are English, German, Italian, Scandinavian and Jewish, plus the vendible and uncritical African, and their political ideal is Lincoln the rail-splitter. The Democrats are mostly Scotch, English, Irish and Welsh, and their hero is Andrew Jackson the skull-splitter.

Newspaper reporters look ahead to a Republican convention with anxiety and fear. They equip themselves in advance with the names of all the hotels in the convention city; they study the floor plans. They know that a man who can attain to the presence of the chairman of the New York delegation in the early morning before nominating day can hear in advance what the delegates are to do.

Toward a Democratic convention these same reporters look with feverish pleasure. They don't worry about the hotels or their floor plans. Nor do they pay much attention to what the chairman of the New York or the Texas delegation may say. For they know the delegates will do their nominating in the open, and then only after turning the convention hall into a panorama of the Battle of the Boyne. This is not because Democrats believe in open covenants, openly arrived at, any more than Republicans do, but because a hotel room is too small for a good fight, and, if the public doesn't hear every damaging word said about the final choice of the convention, free speech is attainted and Thomas Jefferson betrayed.

The Ku Klux Klan fight at Madison Square Garden was typical of the sort of thing that could never or only rarely, happen among Republicans. It was brought to a head by exploiting politicians in both factions. Their considerations were neither poetical nor sentimental, for it is in the body of Democratic delegates, not among the professional leaders, that the beautiful Celtic lust for a fight is paramount. The professional politicians of all parties are alike and will compromise for victory on any terms.

Klan representatives in the South and West selected McAdoo as the least likely of all the Democratic candidates to interfere with their activities. They chose him also on the equally accurate estimate that his candidacy offered them the best chance to prevent the nomination of the governor of New York, a Catholic. This strategy became known in the North and East, and the Catholic and anti-Klan Democrats began to mass against it. They chose to support Governor Smith on the correct assumption that his candidacy offered the best chance to prevent the nomination of McAdoo. The revelations that McAdoo had been in the employ of Doheny; that he had remained in that employ after the Doheny-Fall scandal; that he had resigned it only when he had been summoned to testify at Washington; that he had not spoken out frankly when questioned by the committee and by his supporters in mass-meeting at Chicago about the million-dollar Mexican contingent fee — these revelations, in February, seemed to have stopped his candidacy completely, and the joyous preparations for a holy war were suspended. But McAdoo although his defeat if nominated had become obvious, continued his preparations and held his friends to their promise to support him, meanwhile declining to disclaim the open support of the Klan. This brought him to Madison Square Garden the actual candidate of the night-shirted patriots.

The New York *World*, which for a year had been trying to remove the Klan issue by inducing all conventions and candidates to denounce it, had, immediately upon the disclosure of the Doheny connection, declared McAdoo unavailable. But McAdoo declined to accept the rating and called on his friends to rout the *World*, and the North and the East with it. Those who were for him because of the Klan and those who were for him in spite of the Klan now joined forces and encamped in New York under the guns of the *World*. It soon became obvious that the sentiment to denounce the Klan in the platform was too strong to be defeated. Half the cause of convention warfare was about to be eliminated; the *World* did not insist on naming the Klan; and true Democrats began to be disgusted at the prospect of having half their bows and spears taken away from them.

Then in stepped a practical politician with a practical idea, and when he had forced it upon those few Eastern seaboard leaders who were for Al Smith for sentimental and not professional reasons, as howling a battle broke loose as any Democrat could ask, and Smith, McAdoo, the Klan, the antis, the wets, the drys and moderates all lay prostrate on the field. The practical politician was George Brennan of Chicago. His practical idea was this: There isn't going to be any fight over a Klan plank. The lack of a fight may put McAdoo across. Even if it doesn't, I need some extra excitement to carry my county ticket at home. We can get that excitement out of an insistence that the Klan be mentioned by name. It will help

Tammany carry New York for its local ticket. It will help Frank Hague in Jersey and Joe Guffey in Pennsylvania. It will help me in Chicago. If the whole thing does Al Smith good, so much the better. If it does him harm, too bad. But we have got to hold our local forts.

So on this foundation — at least I shall always believe so, and no amount of protestations on Brennan's part of how he loves religious liberty can change my opinion — the bitter, foolish, bloody, devastating war was joined. McAdoo had laid its foundations by suffering Klan support gladly and permitting his cause and that of the Klan to be inextricably woven before the convention met. Brennan had erected the superstructure, filled the edifice with delegates and then set off the bomb. When the debris ceased to fall, somebody looked underneath the pile and dragged out John W. Davis, who then showed that he was not in his right mind by extricating Charles W. Bryan. And Davis confirmed the fact that he was a gassed casual by putting his hand and that of Bryan's into the warm and honest, but weak and faltering, clasp of Clem L. Shaver and, with the bland smile of a Chinese angel, going forth among the electorate for incredible slaughter.

The convention, by a vote or two furnished through the feudal system still prevailing in Georgia, had refused to name the Klan, but had denounced it by definition. So Davis went to New Jersey, where the Klan was weak, and lashed it with the velvet and wire whips of his faultless diction. Huzzah! shouted the noble and the good. What will Coolidge do? Then Davis went to Indiana, where the Klan was strong, and although it was the sole issue between the parties, he didn't mention it at all. This was of no importance, save to the noble and the good, and they never carry elections anyhow. They were disillusioned as to the forthrightness of Davis, and were not so certain that, in Indiana, he wasn't using the same strategy that Coolidge had followed everywhere. But they have illusions to spare, and so they went out and got some more for 1928.

A sad tale? The recital of wasted opportunities, of scheming and conscienceless politicians, of betrayed delegates, of befuddled candidates, of bright dreams shattered and the nation undone? Not at all. For I verily believe that if George Brennan had not insured the combat over the Klan's name, the delegates would have found something else to justify a family massacre. That high sense of poetry and Irish militancy which makes them adore a fight with one another more than victory over the Republicans, and impels them to stand by their several champions only so long as they continue to lose, would have found some other outlet. Two victories with Wilson had been almost too much for the gallant gossoons. The fact that he was still alive had prevented a real shambles at San Francisco. Here was a chance that could not be foregone.

They are resting now. By the waters of the Tombigbee and the Pecos; on the hills of the Piedmont and the Blue Ridge; on the sidewalks of New York and Boston and Jersey City; and amid the sounds and smells of South Halstead street the Democratic men and women are awaiting the happy event of the inauguration of Calvin Coolidge. Not that directly it means very much to them. But think how a New York Democrat would have felt had the reviewing stand revealed on March 4 the tall, lean figure of McAdoo. And suppose a Kluxian Georgian had been compelled to witness or imagine Tammany marching up Pennsylvania Avenue under the melting gaze of Al Smith!

So hurrah for Coolidge!

HUGH L. KEENLEYSIDE
The American Political Revolution of 1924, *Current History, XXI,* March 1925, pp. 833–840

THE definitive results of the election of Nov. 4, 1924, are now embodied in official reports. They show that the campaign which ended in the re-election of President Coolidge was in no way a remarkable one, except for the existence of a third

party which made a substantial showing. Otherwise the political scene was very much as usual: mechanically organized
parades and ovations, imbecilic oratory, "slush fund" charges,
a comparative lack of well-defined issues, *and general apathy
and detachment on the part of a large percentage of the citizens.*
The Republican campaign was excellently managed, both politically and financially; the Democrats lost their real opportunity in the animosities of the July convention; La Follette's
potency was destroyed by the accusation of radicalism, by the
lack of funds and by the unpopularity of his issues of Government ownership and the Supreme Court. . . .

President Coolidge provided in his personality — whether
real or manufactured — the chief asset in the Republican campaign; and this in spite of his undistinguished record as Vice
President. It was a personal victory, based on a most extraordinary press support. John W. Davis, intellectually one of the
most eminent candidates who ever aspired to the White House,
was unable to unite and revitalize a disorganized and faction-
rent Democracy. Senator Robert M. La Follette, an old school
Western Radical (his ideas are essentially those of the Populist Party of 1890), of high personal character and no little
ability, did not appeal to the South or the East and was finally
deserted even by the Granger States. He failed to organize
either the Farmer or the Labor vote. . . .

LACK OF PUBLIC INTEREST

The lack of popular interest in national campaigns has been
a peculiar, and progressively increasing, characteristic of American political life. In some groups this fact has caused anxiety
as well as curiosity. The passage of the Nineteenth Amendment extended the franchise to more than 25,000,000 politically
inexperienced and in many cases uninterested women. This
has resulted in an increased discrepancy between the number
of eligible and the number of active voters. In 1920, when
less than half the eligible voters actually appeared at the polls,
the cry of "minority government" gave further cause for

serious consideration. In the election of that year, only 26,-711,183 votes were cast out of a possible 54,165,000 — a voting percentage of 49.3. To some persons the success or failure of American democracy appeared to be involved in this situation.

As a result of this condition, the election of 1924 saw a determined effort made by a number of partisan and non-partisan organizations to impress upon all eligible voters the duty, as well as the privilege, embodied in the franchise. For this purpose the National Get-Out-the-Vote League was founded and united in its campaign the American Legion, the National Association of Manufacturers, the various fraternal organizations, the so-called service clubs (Rotary, Kiwanis, and so forth), the National League of Women Voters and State and local committees of varied constitution. On the basis of early returns, officials of many of these organizations issued jubilant statements proclaiming the success of their endeavors. As the official results are tabulated, however, the validity of these claims must be seriously questioned. The election of 1920 was a notoriously dull campaign, and yet the record for 1924, even with the interest created by the third party and the possibility of a Congressional election of the President, raised the percentage of participation less than 2 per cent. Here is little room for jubilation, and the insignificance of the increase becomes even more apparent in the light of the following figures:

Election Year	Number of Eligibles Failing to Vote	Percentage Voting
1896	2,800,000	82.8
1900	5,100,000	77.
1904	6,600,000	67.6
1908	7,200,000	67.
1912	8,800,000	62.8
1916	6,900,000	70.5
1920	27,454,000	49.3
1924	27,819,517	51.1

The condition of a progressively declining participation in government which the above figures portray is undoubtedly a serious one. The real value of the democratic form of government is to be found in its educative effect. Obviously, then, much of the value of American democracy is lost when only 50 per cent. of the citizens partake of its functions. But it is very clear that merely preaching the duty of voting will not have the desired result. This abstract sense of duty needs to be vitalized by a realization of the practical economic benefits to be derived from intelligent voting. The majority of Americans do not yet understand the economic basis of politics or the desirability of voting in accordance with economic needs.

It is a commonplace among political scientists that the two great parties in the United States since 1876, and especially since 1896, have been drawing closer together in doctrine, in practice and in theory. This is the real basis for the lack of interest in national politics. American political life needs a logical division of parties based on economic, geographic and occupational necessities. Such a division will tend to produce an interested, informed and active citizenry. Under present conditions the attempt to "get out the vote" is essentially a useless task.

It should be added that a mere increase in the number of voters is not in itself of major importance. To be of real value it should be accompanied by an increase of *intelligent voting*. The voters need education to such a point that they will no longer be satisfied with the almost complete evasion of all essential issues which has become so characteristic of modern American politics. . . .

The effect of interest on the activity of the voters becomes even more apparent when the sectional division of this vote is examined. The average percentage of eligible voters that actually voted was:

In the Middle Western States	64.8
In the Mountain States	63.1
In the New England States	59.2
In the Pacific Coast States	57.3
In the Middle Atlantic States	53.2
In the Southern States	27.8

These figures show that in the Middle West and Mountain States, where the La Follette campaign was most noisy and active, the greatest interest was aroused and the greatest vote polled. New England, with the first chance in a generation to place a local celebrity in the White House, also was above the average. On the other hand, the solid South, with the election already decided, did not bother to vote,[1] and even the Middle Atlantic States were not particularly interested. (Here the large foreign-born population also had some effect.)

The same principle will be found at work when an examination is made of records of the individual States. The five highest States in percentage of participation were West Virginia 76.8, Indiana 72.3, Utah 71, Wyoming 70.5 and New Hampshire 69.7. Apart from the fact that there is found in these States a great preponderance of native stock, it is also to be considered that West Virginia was voting for or against a native son in a bitter and close election; that Indiana was one of the few Democratic hopes in the West, and that the Ku Klux Klan complicated and vitalized the issue there; that Utah and Wyoming were open fields for any one of the three major candidates, and that New Hampshire was witnessing a bitter Gubernatorial battle, as well as voting to keep a canny New Englander in Washington. As was to have been expected, the States showing the lowest percentage of

---

[1] It should be borne in mind that the real contests in Southern politics take place in the Democratic primaries or nominating conventions. The result of interparty contests is never in doubt and consequently comparatively few persons bother to vote.

participation were found in the South. They were South Carolina 6.3, Georgia 11.3, Mississippi 12.8, Louisiana 13.1 and Alabama 14.3.

As compared with the percentage of active voters in the election of 1920, twenty-six States increased their participation, while twenty-one decreased and one remained constant. The most significant increase came on the Pacific Coast, where Washington, Oregon and California increased their average from 50.4 per cent. to 57.3 per cent. New England increased 3.9 per cent., the Middle West 3.4 per cent. and the Mountain States 2.7 per cent. The Middle Atlantic States decreased .6 per cent. and the Southern States decreased 3.2 per cent. Among the individual States the most notable advances were made by Wyoming 19.1 per cent., California 10 per cent., Nebraska, Oregon, Kansas and Pennsylvania 9 per cent. and Wisconsin 7 per cent. The advance in Pennsylvania is explained by the fact that the Republicans in that State had perhaps the most efficient organization in the history of their party.

The following States showed the most marked decrease: Tennessee 12 per cent., Arizona 11 per cent., Kentucky 9 per cent., Alabama and North Carolina 7 per cent., Virginia, Delaware and Arkansas 6 per cent.

There can be no question that the increased percentage of active voters in the Middle and Far West was produced by La Follette's candidacy; and apparently most of the increase went to him, although it enabled him to win only one State. As the formation and campaign of the Progressive Party were the unique features of the recent campaign, it is advisable at this point to consider their effects.

THE LA FOLLETTE CAMPAIGN

There immediately arises the question as to which of his opponents La Follette struck hardest, and the complementary problem as to whence came his support. Answering the last question first, the explanation is as follows:

La Follette's total vote was 4,820,758. The composition of this total can be determined with reasonable accuracy. In 1920 Eugene Debs, as Socialist candidate, received 919,799 votes. It can hardly be an overstatement, then, to credit Senator La Follette with 1,000,000 Socialist votes. The Progressive vote in the Granger States and on the Pacific Coast was 2,957,570. Estimating the Socialist vote in these States at 425,000 (slightly larger than the Debs vote of 1920), Mr. La Follette can be accredited with what may roughly be called an "agrarian" vote of 2,530,000. The railroad brotherhoods added — outside of the Western states — about 200,000. From these three elements, then, the Progressive total was 3,730,000. This leaves a total of approximately 1,100,000 votes to be divided among Eastern and Southern labor, "liberals" of varied type, and the "protest" vote. Obviously the executive of the American Federation of Labor failed to swing the labor vote to its chosen candidate. The railroad brotherhoods almost alone of organized labor remained constant in allegiance. Their support is evidenced by the winning of Cleveland for La Follette. Union labor failed to follow the advice of the late Mr. Gompers in 1924, as it failed to support his endorsement of Mr. Cox in 1920. How much of this desertion was due to direct or indirect intimidation by conservative employers can never be fully known, but it is safe to explain the greater part of it as a result of the lack of class solidarity on the part of American labor.

It is possible also to judge the effect of the Progressive vote on the two major parties with some assurance. In the election of 1920 the following results were obtained:

Candidate	Per Cent of Total Vote
Harding	60.2
Cox	34.4
Debs and others	5.4

The corresponding results in 1924 were:

Coolidge	54.0
Davis	28.8
La Follette	16.5
Others	.7

It would thus seem that as a result of the Progressive campaign the Republicans suffered a decrease of 6.2 per cent., the Democrats a decrease of 5.6 per cent. and the scattered protest vote of 4.7 percent. The figures are for the country as a whole. It is of interest to compare the figures for 1920 and 1924 in the various sections of the country. For the election of 1920 the percentages were as follows:

States	*Rep.*	*Dem.*	*Others*
Pacific Coast	63.3	25.2	11.2
Mountain	61.4	35.1	3.5
New England	66.1	29.1	4.8
Middle Western	65.1	29.2	5.7
Middle Atlantic	60.5	33.6	5.9
Southern	40.3	55.3	4.4

In 1924 the percentages were changed with the following result:

States	*Rep.*	*Dem.*	*Others*	*La Follette*
Pacific Coast	55.2	10.8	1.5	32.5
Mountain	50.4	21.4	. .	28.2
New England	63.2	26.4	.6	9.8
Middle Western	55.6	23.2	.6	20.6
Middle Atlantic	56.9	29.2	.7	13.2
Southern	34.4	59.1	1.0	5.5

These percentages clearly indicate that La Follette decreased the Republican vote by 8.4 per cent. in the Pacific Coast

States, 11 per cent. in the Mountain States, 2.9 per cent. in New England, 9.5 per cent. in the Middle West, 3.6 per cent. in the Middle Atlantic States and 5.9 per cent. in the South. Similarly he decreased the Democratic vote by 14.4 per cent. on the Pacific Coast, 14.7 per cent. in the Mountain States, 2.7 per cent. in New England, 6 per cent. in the Middle West and 4.4 per cent. on the Atlantic seaboard. In the South the Democratic percentage increased. In other words, the Democratic Party was injured more than the Republican on the Pacific Coast, in the Mountains and in the Atlantic States. The Republicans suffered most in the Middle Western States, in the South and in New England.

From the standpoint of electoral votes, the Progressives appear to have injured the Democrats more than they injured the Republicans. The fear of throwing the election of the President into Congress was perhaps the most potent factor in swelling the Republican vote. President Coolidge was a minority victor in thirteen States (Arizona, Idaho, Kentucky, Maryland, Missouri, Montana, Nebraska, Nevada, New Mexico, North Dakota, South Dakota, Utah and West Virginia). It is probable that at least five of these States would have been won by Mr. Davis in a straight Republican-Democratic contest. Mr. Davis was a minority victor in only one State (Oklahoma).

The Progressive vote was rather more evenly distributed than is generally supposed. Mr. La Follette received 16.8 per cent. of his votes in the Pacific Coast and Mountain States, 29.1 per cent. on the Middle Atlantic Coast, 45.4 per cent. in the Middle West, 4.5 per cent. in New England and 4.2 per cent. in the South. Bearing in mind the relative size of the sections, this is a fairly even distribution, except for New England and the Solid South.

THE FINAL RESULTS

President Coolidge received his vote as follows: 9.9 per cent. in the Pacific Coast and Mountain States, 37.4 per cent. on the Middle Atlantic Coast, 36.6 per cent. in the Middle West, 8.8

per cent. in New England and 7.3 per cent. in the South. Mr. Davis's vote was divided thus: 4.9 per cent. in the Pacific Coast and Mountain States, 35.8 per cent. on the Middle Atlantic Coast, 28.9 per cent. in the Middle West, 6.8 per cent. in New England and 23.6 per cent. in the South. Excluding the solid South,[2] the popular vote for the three major candidates was: Coolidge, 14,576,810; Davis, 6,410,104; La Follette, 4,624,648.

Excluding New England also, the result is: Coolidge, 13,-184,213; Davis, 5,827,194; La Follette, 4,407,056.

Senator La Follette ran first in one State (Wisconsin, where he polled more votes than his combined opponents). He defeated Mr. Davis in eleven States (California, Oregon, Washington, Idaho, Montana, Nevada, Wyoming, North Dakota, South Dakota, Iowa and Minnesota), but ran second to President Coolidge in each.

In the Electoral College President Coolidge won thirty-five States and a vote of 382; Mr. Davis won twelve States and 136 votes; Mr. La Follette, one State and 13 votes. By actual majority vote Coolidge won twenty-two States with 296 votes (only 266 are necessary for election), and his opponents polled a majority in twenty-six States with 235 votes.

The fear of a Congressional election of the President, which characterized the recent campaign, has drawn attention to the archaic methods employed in choosing the Chief Magistrate. It is especially to be hoped that the useless and expensive

---

[2] The belief is rather widely held that with the increase of industrialization the Republican Party is gradually growing stronger, both absolutely and comparatively, in the solid South. A comparison of the results of 1920 and 1924 does not bear this out. In 1924 the Democratic Party polled 95 per cent. of the total number of votes which they received in 1920. The Republican Party polled only 87 per cent. of its 1920 total. The Republicans and Progressives together received 2 per cent. less votes in 1924 than did the Republicans alone in 1920. Both positively and comparatively the Republican strength declined. The Republican vote decreased in every Southern State except New Mexico.

Electoral College will be abolished. A constitutional amendment with this end in view is now before Congress. In the new Congress the parties will appear as follows:

Senate		House	
Republicans	50	Republicans	232
Democrats	40	Democrats	183
Farmer-Labor	1	Farmer-Labor	3
La Follette Republicans	5	Socialist	2
		La Follette Republicans	15

This alignment shows a shrinkage in both Democratic and Progressive ranks. The American Federation of Labor, which checks very closely the social attitudes of Congressional candidates, admits a net loss of two pro-labor Senators and fifteen pro-labor Representatives. If Senator Brookhart should be unseated the Senate loss would be three. The federation endorsed twenty-three candidates for the Senate, of whom fourteen were elected. Of 284 endorsed for the House, 179 were successful. The Democratic Party sustained a net loss of two Senators and twenty-four Representatives. The Farmer-Labor Party lost one Senator, but gained two members in the House. The regular Republicans gained fifteen members in the House and three Senators. . . .

DEMOCRATIC PARTY'S DECLINE

In the light of the preceding analysis, it may now be stated that the national election of 1924 was characterized by: (1) the largest number of votes ever cast in a single election in the history of the world; (2) a slight increase over 1920 in the percentage of eligible voters who exercised their franchise; (3) an increase, both positively and comparatively, in the number of women voters; (4) an extremely light vote in the South and an increase in the agricultural States of the West: (5) the triumph of conservatism; (6) the formation of a new Progressive Party, and (7) the continued retrogression, in the national field, of the Democratic Party.

The last two statements deserve further consideration, for they are undoubtedly the most significant results of the late campaign. If it is true that the election of 1924 is simply another step in the decadence of a once vigorous party, it can only mean one of two things. Either the Democratic Party is dying to make way for another strong national party or else the United States has at last succumbed to the "bloc" system of representative government. A view of the party history of this country since the election of 1896 gives irrefutable proof of the progressively more hopeless situation of the present Democratic Party, and even a cursory study of its present component parts will end any hope for its resurrection and reestablishment as a virile national force.

The year 1896 is chosen because it marks the introduction of the modern era in American political history. The American scene was characterized, in the last decade of the nineteenth century, by the passing of the frontier and its promise of free land, by the beginning of economic imperialism, by the great increase in that South European emigration to the United States which recent laws have sought to stem, by the enormous development of financial organization which has reacted so definitely upon the political system, and, in spite of free silver and Bryanism, this decade saw the beginning of that progressive unification (so far as principle is concerned) of the two major political parties. This complex of forces has produced the modern United States, and in this modern society the Democratic Party has been gradually forced into the background. The following statistics will justify this assertion:

Election	Total Votes	Rep. Per Cent.	Dem. Per Cent.	Others P. C.
1896	13,826,012	51.0	46.8	2.2
1900	13,971,275	52.8	45.9	2.3
1904	13,534,289	56.8	38.0	5.2
1908	14,877,133	52.0	43.3	4.7
1912	15,031,169	$\begin{Bmatrix} 23.5 \\ 27.8 \end{Bmatrix}$ 51.3[3]	45.2	3.5
1916	18,528,743	46.2	49.4	4.4
1920	26,711,183	60.2	34.4	5.4
1924	29,074,804	54.1	28.7	17.2

These statistics make it clear that since 1896 the Democratic Party has been nationally successful twice, that it has defeated the united Republican Party only once[4] and that it has never polled 50 per cent. of the votes in any one election. During that period the Republican Party averaged 53 per cent. of the vote and the Democratic Party 41 per cent. On every occasion, except 1916, the Republican Party has polled over 50 per cent. of the votes cast.

In spite of this record, the Democratic Party might still continue, with some hope of success in periods of Republican strife, if it were a united liberal party. The Republican Party has an apparently unbreakable grip on the conservative element of the country outside the solid South. All the rules of political logic, then, demand that the Democratic Party, to continue as a vital element, should organize and express American liberalism. And this the Democratic Party cannot do because of its Southern elements. It is torn by the strife of irreconcilable

[3] The two sets of figures show the split Republican vote caused by Theodore Roosevelt's secession from the Republican Party.

[4] The election of 1916 was of course a unique phenomenon. The greatly increased vote of that year and the re-election of a Democratic President can only be explained on the basis of a national desire to keep out of the World War. "He kept us out of war" was barely sufficient to carry the election for President Wilson and the Democrats.

forces — the aristocratic ultra-conservative South, the predominantly Catholic, foreign-born, working class elements of the Northeast, and a rapidly diminishing strength among the farmers and proletariat of the Middle and Far West. The strife between these discordant elements is growing more bitter instead of less.

In the face of this record, it must be conceded that the historic Democratic Party can now barely qualify as a national force and that its progressive disintegration is almost assured. What will take its place — another party, national, liberal and united, or a system of blocs?

"BLOC" GOVERNMENT FORESHADOWED

Recognizing as one must the extraordinary power of the two-party tradition in American politics, it must be conceded that the present outlook rather presages bloc government. It may be possible for the liberal elements in the two old parties to unite with organized labor, (the sine qua non of a liberal movement which hopes to succeed) in a strong national party, but every sign is against it; most particularly the political innocence of the laboring groups. This is, however, the hope of those who organized and supported the Progressive Party of 1924.

The modern United States is now a complex of many and antagonistic groups, and the basis of this division is economic. It would seem probable, then, that this Republic is about to follow the lead of every other mature State and hand over the control of its destinies to a combination of political blocs. These blocs will be based upon the economic needs of their respective geographic or class constituencies. For a country of the size and diversity of the United States no other development can be expected. How this will be accomplished is another problem.

CHAPTER 3

Persistent
Political Issues
of the Twenties

A running battle between Congress and the executive branch began in 1921 and lasted through the ten years of the decade. Republican control of both houses neither assured support for policies advanced by such key administration leaders as Secretary of State Charles Evans Hughes and Secretary of Treasury Andrew W. Mellon nor did it prevent important Congressional proposals that ran counter to the wishes of the executive departments. This chapter gathers commentaries on four of the important political issues of the twenties. In each there were important disagreements between executive and legislative branches.

Of the four issues, one, the Immigration Act of 1924, was approved but contained provisions that had been resisted by Secretary of State Hughes and President Coolidge. Two were stalemated: vetoes by President Coolidge ended the long quest for farm relief through regulation of marketing; the question of how to dispose of the power facilities at Muscle Shoals remained on the legislative agenda in 1933. The fourth, the Mellon tax plan, was twice seriously qualified in Congress and was finally approved in 1926 substantially in the form it had been proposed only because Democrats in Congress deserted their Progressive allies.

A. RELIEF FOR THE AMERICAN FARMER

The nation's farm market, overexpanded because of wartime demands for American products abroad, collapsed in 1921 and an agricultural depression began that continued until the nineteen thirties. In May, 1921, at the instigation of the newly formed American Farm Bureau Federation, a group of farm state Congressmen took the initiative to expedite farm legislation. Out of this grew a "Farm Bloc" that embraced about 20 Senators and 100 Representatives. The most important achievements of the 67th Congress, 1921–1923, were the results of their pressure. The farm bloc was a sectional coalition, most successful when it could bind Congressmen representing the cotton South with those from corn and wheat producing areas of the middle West. It cut across party lines and included Progressives like Senators George Norris of Nebraska, Robert M. La Follette of Wisconsin, William E. Borah of Idaho, and Smith W. Brookhart of Iowa, but it also included conservative Southern Democrats like "Cotton Ed" Smith of South Carolina and distinctly non-Progressive Republicans like Arthur Capper of Kansas and Representative (later Senator) L. J. Dickinson from Iowa.

The major farm proposal of the twenties, the McNary-Haugen Bill, was designed to give the farmer a "fair exchange" value for his products based upon what the ratio of farm prices to farm costs had been before the war. This would be achieved by freeing farmers from the price depressing effects of the world market. A high tariff would exclude most foreign commodities. A two price system would be created whereby products consumed domestically would be marketed at the "fair exchange value," surplus beyond domestic needs would be "dumped" by the government abroad at the prevailing world price. An equalization fee assessed against participating farmers would recoup the government's losses and an individual farmer would gain to the extent his return minus the equalization fee was greater than the world price. The bill, supported by the Farm Bureau and most farm organizations, came before Congress four times. It was defeated in the House in 1924 and lost in both houses in 1926. It passed Congress in 1927 and again in 1928 when the vote was 53–23 in the Senate and 204–121 in the House. The bill succeeded in 1927 and 1928 because Southern Congressmen, prompted by the mounting depression in cotton areas, swung to its support in sufficient numbers to pass it. The McNary-Haugen Bill ran counter to the economic principles and the more restricted proposals for agricultural reform of the Republican administration, particularly Secretary of Commerce Herbert Hoover. President Coolidge twice vetoed the bill.

In the first of two quite different analyses of the farm problem of the twenties, Senator Arthur Capper, a major leader of the farm bloc, chronicles the coalition's early achievements. When he writes, "Unless the farmer prospers there can be no prosperity of a single industry," Capper is invoking a tradition of "agricultural fundamentalism" that has a venerable place in American history. In contrast, Rexford Tugwell, professor of economics at Columbia University, views the farm problem of the twenties in terms of long range prospects for American agriculture. In this context he finds the McNary-Haugen plan deficient since it provided no means for reducing the price depressing surplus. Tugwell was to have an opportunity to expedite his solution when he served Franklin D. Roosevelt as a member of the "brainstrust" in 1933 and subsequently as Undersecretary of Agriculture.

ARTHUR CAPPER

The Agricultural Bloc — Its Merits, *The Forum, LXVI, December 1921, pp. 461–470*

Criticism of the so-called agricultural bloc in the present Congress as a "class group" has come, so far as I have observed, from class groups who fear recognition of the primary national industry by the government. These men in Congress, comprising about one hundred in the House and some twenty-two in the Senate, largely from the west and south, who know the needs of agriculture, are accused by representatives of other interests of seeking class legislation for the farm.

The legislation which the agricultural bloc supports as its contribution to the general welfare, however, speaks for itself. As one who has actively supported and advocated these measures, I have no sympathy with class legislation, and I need hardly say that I see nothing of the evils of class legislation in the agricultural program.

It is trite to say that "agriculture is the basis of our prosperity." But threadbare as the statement is, it has needed repetition and emphasis. At the base of all industry is the oldest industry of the land itself. We may say that until quite recent years we regarded the farmer as valuable in his capacity as a producer of the first needs of life, but all great business now equally considers him as purchaser. He produces the raw material for the factory and he supports the factory in his immense

consumption of finished products. Our entire business structure rests upon the land. The farmer not only feeds us and
clothes us, but is, as a class, our best customer. Without him
the railroads would languish. The steel industry, without the
railroad demand for rails and other materials, and the demand
of the harvester and farm implement industries for steel, would
perish. Unless the farmer prospers there can be no prosperity
of a single industry. So efforts to improve and stabilize production are of as vital consequence to the city and to business
in general as to the farmer himself.

Heretofore government aid to agriculture has consisted in
the support of agricultural colleges and experiment stations,
and the Department of Agriculture. Valuable as this service
has been in promoting better farming, improved seed, soil culture and livestock, it has no relation to other and increasingly
pressing problems of the farming industry which concern such
subjects as financial credit and markets, and marketing machinery and processes.

Farming is a peculiar industry. It has not participated in the
modern synthetical processes of industrialism, the centralization
of control, the combination of capital into great units. In the
immense development of the division of labor in the factory
system and through the corporation, agriculture has been left
by the wayside. It remains as individualistic as a century ago,
when all industrialism was individualistic. The farmer is the
sole survivor of an earlier industrial order, when the shoe-
maker made shoes on his knee in his shop, when domestic industry flourished, and the household spun its own wool and
was sufficient unto itself. With the development of the factory
system and the corporation, and the corresponding evolution
of credit and banking with relation to these new forms, agriculture has been overlooked. Farming is the only business
left that buys at retail and sells at wholesale; that pays what is
asked when it buys, and accepts what is offered when it sells.
The farmer remains merely a producer of the necessaries of
human life. After he has produced them other organizations

take them over at their own price for distribution. This is true of no other important industry.

The marketing and distributing agencies, well supplied with credit, closely affiliated and linked with the highly organized industrial order, do not, like the farmer, dump the farmer's products, after they have passed into their hands, at once upon a congested market. Facilities have grown up, the warehousing system, the elevator, the cold storage plant, the grain, cotton and other exchanges, that nicely adjust supply to demand, and the "middlemen" feed out the world's food supplies as demand calls for them. Just as these merchants hold and store and distribute in accordance with demand for consumption, thereby obtaining what the products are fairly worth during the entire year, so the farmer is now proposing through self-organization to dispose of his products, to control elevators, warehouses, credit, to be represented on exchanges, to market his own products. This is the first agricultural bloc aid to the farmer, in the Volstead-Capper bill authorizing farm co-operative marketing.

The farmer's individualistic industry, the single farm being the unit, not the corporate aggregation of many farms, is not adapted to the uses of the modern corporation. What is suited to agriculture (unless it is to be taken over bodily by big business in great trusts) is co-operation. There is not an economist nor an authority on agriculture who believes that the method of the corporation will answer the needs of agriculture. Co-operation differs from the corporation in several important features, but it is unnecessary to mention more than that in co-operation the amount of stock shall be limited to any one stockholder to the co-operative project, and the stock dividends shall be limited to a fixed rate having no relation to the earnings, as in the corporation, but having regard to the ruling rate of interest for money or capital. Only by these limitations can the farm marketing enterprise be protected against control by a few, and the vital co-operative spirit maintained. In co-operation capital and labor are one. The farmer supplies the capital and it is he who turns out the product. The ultimate earnings dividends are rated not on the capital invested, but on the product contributed. This is true co-operation.

What the agricultural bloc discovered is that existing "middlemen" through their organizations are determined to prevent the rise of farm co-operative marketing. Aspiring local co-operative organizations of farmers were attacked by these interests in the courts for violation of the anti-trust acts, and co-operation was obstructed and discouraged by these and other measures.

Convinced that farm co-operation is desirable, the last Congress by an amendment of the federal trade act undertook to release it from any suspicion of attempted monopoly by exempting combinations "not for profit" from the scope of the anti-trust acts, acts designed for wholly different forms of organization. The amendment proved ineffective, and the Volstead-Capper bill now being pressed by the agricultural bloc, authorizes and validates farm co-operation as such. . . .

In clearing the way for farm co-operation the agricultural bloc is not seeking to give a special advantage to the farmer over other industrialists, but to open the way for the farmer to adopt a plan of industrial organization as suited to the conditions of his industry, as the corporation is suited to others. Other measures to which the so called farm bloc has given its sanction include the Capper-Tincher anti-grain gambling bill already enacted into law. This is a measure, not of class legislation, but of correction of abuses on grain exchanges. It abolishes the practice of "puts" and "calls," condemned by grain exchanges themselves and many years ago prohibited in their own rules. But the main provisions of the bill give the Secretary of Agriculture power to investigate and report any suspected manipulation of the grain market, to check the books of market operators, and to prescribe rules for boards of trade. Other measures included are Senator Dial's anti-cotton gambling bill, bills regulating cold storage and providing control of the packing industry, the Capper-French truth in fabrics bill — applying to fabrics provisions similar to those of the pure food act — and bills creating more liberal banking credit, particularly personal credit on crops and farm machinery, making such paper more easily discountable.

Of these measures the only one susceptible to the accusation of "class legislation" is the last, since it does attempt to enlarge the banking credit of agriculture. People in cities or engaged in mercantiles, manufacturing, brokerage or other business associated with cities are not aware of the extent to which bank credit has been evolved with relation to the needs specifically of such industries, and the extent to which the evolution of bank credit has overlooked the peculiar conditions of agriculture.

Commercial paper is the key of banking credit. Credit machinery and facilities have accommodated themselves to the needs of commercial and manufacturing business. Since this business ordinarily has a turnover measured in weeks, bank credit has adapted itself to such periods of duration and renewal. We have the thirty day, sixty day, and at most ninety day note, and this arrangement perfectly suits commercial business. In fact that is the reason we have it. It does not suit farming business, yet this fact has not in the least modified the practice, demonstrating conclusively that bank credit does not concern itself seriously with the industry of the production of the world's food supply. The farmer's turnover is mainly once in twelve months. Furthermore, the supply of bank credit has no relation to agriculture, but regards commercial and manufacturing business only. The banks have mainly concerned themselves with supplying the credit needs of "business," in which farm business is not consciously included. But even so, the banks have not adequately met the need of commercial business. This appears by the development of one auxiliary credit organization after another. We have the discount companies or commercial credit companies that buy accounts receivable of merchants and manufacturers to increase mercantile and manufacturing working capital.

These modern institutions of very recent creation now do an extensive business of auxiliary banking for the benefit of business in cities. Of recent origin too, are the commercial banking departments of trust companies, under more liberal regulation than banks, created to meet the demands of commercial and manufacturing industry. And finally we have the commercial paper houses. According to Prof. H. G. Moulton of Chicago University, in his book recently from the press, "The Financial Organization of Society," these last did a business in 1919 of upwards of four billion dollars. They are an extension of the facilities of bank credit for the special benefit of merchants and manufacturers, and their particular function is to find the widest market, often even in the small country or farm bank, for the paper of great commercial houses.

But where do we see any extension of bank credit that helps the farmer finance his business? He has paid the highest interest rate for working capital, not because his credit is naturally inferior to that of commercial business, but because the banking system has grown up in places and under conditions remote from those of farm industry.

It is not the purpose of the agricultural bloc in the banking credit measures they advocate, to supply the farmer with a more generous line of credit than other industries, but to fill the wide gap that has existed between his industry and the credit that all other industry enjoys. It is merely a belated effort to meet a profound need of agriculture. The purpose of the credit bills is to create banking facilities for the farmer adjusted to the times and seasons of his need, not to give credit where credit is not warranted. The bills provide for ample security for any credit the farmer asks, but they take notice of the longer period of his business turnover both as to crops and as to livestock. The farmer in the past has had the credit facilities only of the little country bank. The agricultural bloc was instrumental in obtaining the enactment of the agricultural credit bill, through which a maximum of one billion dollars credit may be extended to farm loan organizations and to banks and trust companies making loans to farmers, and through which the War Finance Corporation may make advances not exceeding one year to producers or dealers in the event of a market glut, and may advance credit to any co-operative association, bank or trust company which has advanced funds for agricultural purposes, as well as credit for the breeding, fattening and marketing of livestock.

Many Americans give little thought to the agricultural industry. It is removed from the populous centers of the country. The farmer is isolated, he stands alone, the last of the individualists, depending for his success upon his own efforts unassociated with others. Yet he conducts an industry aggregating an investment value of eighty billion dollars, and with a normal output of something like twenty billions. He is "fed up" on political camouflage and promises, on Fourth of July oratory extolling his loyalty, his industry, his patience, and his fidelity to his job. He is weary of hearing that he is the "backbone" of the country, its "bone and sinew," only to be forgotten when business is to be done and results harvested. He is asking for a square deal and equal treatment and consideration with others, for the right to act in co-operation and to handle his products through to their ultimate market, with adequate credit facilities. Oratorically the farmer has been well treated. Practically his needs have been neglected by those who have made the laws and the modern machinery of the industrial order. He has awakened to his own situation. When the after-war collapse occurred it was the farmer who was without the organization and machinery to protect himself, and he saw his products made the football of speculation and gambling.

When an eighty billion dollar industry capable of supplying the nation annually with twenty-two billions of new wealth, and fifty per cent of its bank deposits, lies flat on its back, it would seem that rescue parties might better be hailed with joy than viewed with alarm, and that whatever will promote the primary industry of food production might well be regarded as of the common good, rather than as class legislation and a menace.

Nobody can impartially study the history of agriculture and conclude that it has not been sorely neglected. It has "just growed." For a century and a half, nearly everything we have done, every system we have contrived in marketing, transportation and banking, has been built to fit the development, happiness, and profit of city life. A Department of Agriculture and a few agricultural colleges have been regarded as meeting our obligations to agriculture. And so they would, if all that agriculture needed was advice. But it needs to grow and prosper in organized efficiency like the rest of the modern, highly organized world.

In central Illinois, the heart of the most fertile agricultural region on the globe, more farmers have gone bankrupt and been sold out by the sheriff in the last year than in many preceding years together. One of the most successful and respected farmers in the United States, J. R. Howard, president of the American Farm Bureau Federation, has declared that one and a half million of the six million farmers of the country are today insolvent. Agriculture is sick. The measures supported by the agricultural bloc are not proposals to give the farmer something for nothing, nor are they class legislation. They are the remedies urged by economists and students of agriculture, and above all by the farmers themselves, to uplift this fundamental industry to a place where it will be a blessing to the country because it is self sustaining and prosperous.

REXFORD   TUGWELL
Reflections on Farm Relief, *Political Science Quarterly, XLIII,*
December 1928, pp. 481–497
Reprinted with permission of the Political Science Quarterly.

The problem of farm relief presents sharply defined short-
and long-run phases. Both are legitimate fields for governmental
research and legislative intervention. That is to say, something
can be done. But whatever is done about either ought to be
thought of not only in itself but with reference to the other.
The problems are distinct, but their solutions would necessarily
have mutual significance.

The long-run problem is that of reorganizing the industry,
raising its technical efficiency, reducing its costs, conserving
the social interest in the land — generally enabling the industry
to stand on its own feet among our other more typical ones.
Other businesses are required to direct their efforts toward
reducing their costs and prices. Farmers are now in the embarrassing position of resenting cost-reducing technical advice
and running to the government for help in increasing their
prices. This would not be tolerated in any other occupation,
and, in the long run, it ought not to be permissible for agriculture. It will not be necessary ultimately, however, if the
technical services of the Department of Agriculture, of schools
and experimental farms, are kept at their present effective
level, and if some means of coöperative effort develops gradually out of its promising beginnings. The one will increase
technical proficiency; the other will make farming a large-
scale bargaining — if not producing — industry.

The short-run problem is that of forgetting, for the moment,
all this long, serious, fundamental reorganizing effort, and of
liquidating a present bankruptcy; to give price-relief without
thinking of reduced costs and prices. We have to think of it
as increasing farmers' incomes at the expense, if necessary, of
losses to the consumers of their goods. It ought not to be said

that this process will not involve a social cost. It will; but not so much, perhaps, as its opponents would have us think. Nevertheless there will be a cost and the question is whether it will be worth the sacrifice.

The controversies of recent years have rather tended to obscure the distinctions between these two problems. Emergency relief, especially, has been erected into a consumers' bogey-man of inflated proportions, assumed to be a permanent burden, and the work of those agencies which would strengthen the industry for the long pull has been deliberately ridiculed by those who overemphasized the significance of surpluses. As a result the emergent legislative plans — the McNary-Haugen Bills — have not been entirely satisfactory from either point of view. As long-run measures, they ignored the necessity for technical reorganization and the reduction of costs, assuming, apparently, that at no price would consumers use more farm products, and that surpluses are to be gauged by the amounts of unsold products at present prices. Furthermore, in establishing profitable prices, they presented no definite — or, at least, enforceable — means for keeping down recurrent surpluses of increasing size. The difficulties attending the effort to market more and more goods at high prices are obvious. As short-run measures, even, there were objectionable features — such, for instance, as dependence upon a non-existent universal coöperative organization amongst farmers themselves, as the basic member-units of the system.

Another difficulty, which seems very real indeed, is that the program, as it came to be framed in legislation, appealed only to a limited number of farmers themselves: those whose products go heavily into export — mostly cotton, wheat and tobacco growěrs. A farmer in the East or Middle West, with a rounded mixed farming routine, can see little gain from a plan which depends for its success upon the manipulation of exports. Many farm products have an almost wholly domestic sale. Consequently, dairying, fruit-growing, vegetable-gardening, stock-raising, or even corn- or hog-producing farmers are not enthusiastic believers in McNary-Haugenism.

Division in farmers' councils has been apparent from the first. And they never have succeeded in establishing agreement among themselves. The legislation as it emerged represented the dominant ideas of wheat and cotton growers rather than others; but it lost much of its appeal from lack of enthusiasm among large groups with other dominant producing interests. Not only this. Also contributing to the division has been the fact that the long-drawn-out depression affected certain regions more than others. One measure of this situation is changes in land values. For the prices paid for land are a most constant and burdensome obligation. Mortgages have to be met and interest, meantime, has to be paid. Land acquired at a relatively low price made, for many Eastern farmers, a relatively easy recovery from the depression years. The low prices they received were far from acceptable; but fewer of them were actually unable to meet their obligations. In states such as Kansas or Iowa, where land-speculation raised the values of land to impossible earning levels, the depression had more disastrous consequences. As a result the farmers in those regions have been most clamorous for Federal relief.

Yet there are few farmers in the whole country who do not carry an intense grievance, a feeling of having been unjustly treated. As Mr. Bliven remarked in 1922, they have followed all the copy-book maxims, have been hard-working, honest, persistent, but nevertheless, social forces beyond their control have constantly threatened them — and sometimes they have been swamped. Specifically they know that theirs is a business which, on the whole, has no money in it. Their estimated losses last year, allowing each proprietor a wage of fifteen hundred dollars, would be not much less than six billion dollars. And they are finding out all these facts. They want something done. But most of them are still unconvinced that the right scheme has been advanced. No general assent to any program has as yet been gained.

Economists have a generally accepted rule that an increase in the supply of staple goods — such as farm products are — will cause prices to fall in a degree entirely disproportionate to the size of the increase. The stimulations of war noticeably increased our farm production; but the war-time markets shrunk as soon as European farm activity was resumed, and when credits began to falter under continued inflation. The American market was suddenly required to absorb the unusual amounts which had been flowing out as exports. But this primary cause for the crisis of 1920 was made worse — deliberately, farm leaders say — by the forced deflation of credits which began at the height of the marketing season.

Farm products could only be sold at a ruinous disadvantage; nevertheless they had to go for what they would bring, for there were pressing obligations to meet. In the regions of conspicuous land speculation the total receipts for several years were not large enough even to pay interest on mortgages. But foreclosure was unsatisfactory even for creditors. The land simply could not earn enough in any hands to meet the charges upon it. Frozen credits, chronic bankruptcy, lasting for years, followed the *débâcle*. Liquidation is just now being completed. And just now the purchasing power of farm products has reached the pre-war level. A burnt child fears the fire, however, and farmers now, though their present ills are less, fear another disastrous turn of the wheel. Furthermore, they are no longer satisfied with pre-war conditions. Their complaints have by now become more organized, leaders have appeared, and there is voting strength in the bloc to be reckoned with. They are disposed to seek a settlement now, while their political bargaining strength is unimpaired.

Eight years of gradually liquidating depression have incalculably injured the nation's agricultural plant. Fertility has been depleted, equipment has run down, man-power has deteriorated. Not only farmers themselves, but all thoughtful social observers are seriously concerned that some ingenuity and some public action should be enlisted and at once. At best farming suffers needless handicaps. Back to 1913 is not good enough. For, strictly speaking, what happened between 1920 and 1928 is nothing new in our history. Indeed a more or less organized agrarian revolt is nothing new. If we were to look backward we should see that each of those phenomena we call the business cycle and which, in Europe, they call the economic rhythm, has had similar consequences for rural folks. The characteristic course of the general price level through one of these cyclical movements can be idealized [as a bell curve].

But if, from the general price indexes, those of agricultural and non-agricultural goods were abstracted and super-imposed, there would be found to be regularly recurring differences in behavior.

. . . When prices move upward, those of agriculture gradually gain on others and finally show an advantage, which, however, is rapidly lost when the turn comes. The disadvantage of farmers is measured roughly by the fact that they lose more in depression than they gain in prosperity, and that this continues to be true, with a periodical exploitation of those engaged in this activity for the benefit of those engaged in other pursuits.

This, perhaps, gives us the best key we can get to the immediate problem of farm-relief. . . . it might be said that the real problem which must be faced by those who would do something genuine and immediate for farmers is to insure a price-relationship between agricultural and non-agricultural products which will be constant.

The McNary-Haugen idea was that this price disparity, recurrently so disastrous, might be traced to the economic rule that small surpluses have disproportionate effects on prices and that this situation might be relieved by the segregation of this small percentage which has such great consequences. It might then be disposed of safely in either of two ways: storage or export. Coöperative storage, assisted by government financing, might enable farmers to wait for favorable markets. At least marketing could be spread throughout the year. Dumping abroad, with proper management of import duties, could be done at any price, provided the elimination of the surplus was complete; for then domestic prices could be kept at a level which would yield a profit on the whole of any crop. This device, it was argued, would at last admit farmers to the American protective system on an equality with other industries.

A stabilization fund would be set up by the government; equalization fees, assessed against the products to be marketed, would prevent its dissipation and locate the costs of operation where they belonged. All this was not to function as individual help to farmers; they were supposed first to set up local and regional coöperative associations with power to do business for their members. Government financial aid was to be extended for assistance in organizing these bodies as well as for insuring against loss of profits in marketing.

All this was objected to by Mr. Coolidge as unconstitutional and as administratively impossible. There is doubt as to constitutionality, but it is only doubt; and that decision belongs to the courts. As to the complexity of administration, this is a charge which might be brought against almost any governmental device. Simplicity is desirable, but lack of it ought not to prevent the adoption of a desirable policy. Besides, the scheme, if complex, was necessarily so. It may be better to do something difficult than to do nothing at all. His real objection was a stubborn determination to do nothing. New England minds revolt against any economic proposal which is more socially oriented than Vermont shop-keeping. But the veto stood.

The scheme seemed workable enough, and administratively possible, provided only that foreign governments made no retaliatory moves to protect their own farmers, and that the surpluses in question did not grow so big, with profit insurance, as to prove unwieldy. But obviously it applied mostly to exportable (or easily stored)products; and, quite as obviously it depended upon a huge coöperative organization among farmers of which only the barest beginnings were to be discerned.

President Harding seems to have been considerably shaken when, in 1921, he ran onto the fact that making goods does not always involve making money, especially in agricultural occupations. In his message to Congress he stated the problem:

It is rather shocking to be told, and to have the statement strongly supported, that nine million bales of cotton, raised on American plantations in a given year, will actually be worth more to the producers than thirteen million bales would have been. Equally shocking is the statement that seven hundred million bushels of wheat, raised by American farmers, would bring them more money than a billion bushels. Yet these are not exaggerated statements. In a world where there are tens of millions who need food and clothing which they cannot get, such a condition is sure to indict a social system which makes it possible.

In strict logic, this last sentence may seem something of a *non sequitur*. Yet, in a way, it does follow that something is wrong in a social system whose mechanisms discourage productivity when there are those who are in need of food and clothing. The Agricultural Conference which was called to solve this problem helped very little. No one there wanted to do anything drastic; and no one had any ideas. The question, why, when there are people in need, will they pay only as much for a small crop as they will for a large one, goes pretty deep. The answer to it does constitute an indictment of our arrangements. But the defenders of those arrangements have managed, so far, to fight off any corrective surgery. It became progressively more difficult to do so, however, as continued discussion clarified the facts and sharpened the issues. We came within an inch of stringent change this last year. And if the camel's nose once gets under the tent, institutions of many another industry may find themselves let in for an overhauling.

Mr. Coolidge inherited the puzzle of farmers penalized for productivity. But puzzles do not worry him. Besides he held

it certain that prosperity would recur in his time to justify in-
action. The obstinate persistence of the farm leaders in pointing
out the remarkable duration of the depression and the certainty
of its recurrence has annoyed him, but not unbearably. His
last McNary-Haugen veto lacked something of aplomb; it
was even sharp. But it may be doubted whether it satisfied
everyone that the economics of New England shopkeeping is
adequate to the solution of the difficulty.

Meantime we have been achieving a much better notion of
why it is that large crops carry penalties, and something of an
idea concerning a remedy. For now it seems that President
Harding, though he touched a distressing fact, did not explore
it far enough. The addition to be made is this: though there
may be cold and hungry people in the world, they may not be
able to pay as much for cotton or for wheat as is required to
meet the cost of production in Mississippi or in Oregon. The
number of those who both desire to buy and possess the where-
withal may be limited to the number who will absorb nine millions of bales of cotton and seven hundred million bushels of
wheat. This ought, of course, to condemn any social system.
Yet we cannot quite set out to solve the American crop-surplus
problem by raising the buying power of all the world's people.
Urban poverty is a social disease which cannot legitimately
find its cure in an alternative poverty for rural folk.

If we are mainly interested in relief for American farmers,
our problem is far simpler than that. It is, in fact, the problem of producing only as much as consumers can afford to buy
at a price somewhat above the cost of production. Anything
more than this is the surplus about which we hear so much,
and which, whatever else we may say of it, indubitably possesses a disproportionate power to smash prices. Given a
twenty-five per cent surplus, farmers with pressing obligations
will find themselves forced to sell far below their actual costs.
They have done it year after year.

It is true that, if we consider ourselves obligated to consumers as well as to producers, we shall not be content with a program of restricted production. For more could undoubtedly be sold at lower prices; and lower prices could still be profitable if costs could be reduced. The long-run problem is this: to increase efficiency, lower costs, reduce prices, widen markets, and feed and clothe more people at less expense. But the reorganization of agriculture cannot start there. For such a program requires immense research and extensive capital outlay. Capital will not flow into an unprofitable industry. It will not even stay there, such of it as can be got out by its owners. The first step is to make farming profitable. And for this it is necessary to adjust production to the amount which will be consumed at prices which are higher than present (not future) costs.

The problem of immediate farm relief is, then, that of limiting production, not to the nation's or the world's needs, but to the buying capacity of the farmer's market. Do this to begin with and other desirable results may follow.

But how shall we limit production? This is difficult to say; and every proposal seems to have difficulties. If they are not administrative or fiscal, they are constitutional. The simplest scheme would seem to be one which would contain the following elements:

(1) A survey of the amounts necessary to meet normal needs and which will command a profitable price.

(2) Notice of limitation of planting, on a basis of ten-year averages, by local (probably county) agents of a Farm Board.

(3) Enforcement through denial of the use of railways and warehouses to produce grown on unauthorized acreage.

The steel manufacturers or the milk distributors of the country could not carry out such a scheme for themselves, much less enlist governmental assistance. What excuse is there for either permitting farmers to do it or assisting in the venture?

Merely that this is genuinely the kind of thing which the Supreme Court before now has recognized as a "controlling emergency." Our agricultural plant is deteriorating; it not only makes no progress but rapidly wastes away. We must save it by heroic means; and if we must break all our precedents, why not go straight to what we know is the root of the matter, limit production, make the industry profitable, then watch it develop once more as an independent art?

There has been too little attention paid to the somewhat curious changes in price relationships in recent years. As a matter of fact consumers pay relatively as much for food products and buy relatively as many as they did in 1913. If farmers were well off then, one would say, they ought to be prosperous now. The difficulty is that, though consumers pay as much, farmers do not receive as much. An unusual — and apparently growing — amount is absorbed somewhere between farmer and consumer.

Then, of course, farmers were not well off in 1913. They had grounds for complaint even then. But the situation has been made worse by stealing from their incomes by middlemen. It is sometimes argued that this is the whole trouble: that there is not a surplus, and that surplus-control legislation is therefore not needed. The answer to this is that surpluses existed even before the war; but then contrasts in living standards were less tormenting. The surplus is not greater now, but it is more important. Farmers, years ago, went to the store for fewer goods, and did not feel the need of so many of them. The surplus and low prices therefore meant less in their lives. What they provided for themselves was not affected. But low cash prices mean more and more all the time. Money must be had; farmers are, therefore, more at the mercy of middlemen — both in buying and in selling. And it is more important that surpluses should be controlled than it used to be. It is more important because it equalizes the farmers' monopoly situation with that of those with whom he must deal. It might, or so it seems to some farm leaders, do something needful in an economic way which he cannot possibly do for himself.

Much objection to surplus-control legislation has centered about the equalization fee. It is difficult to see why. If the government is to do anything in the way of assisting in agricultural control, it seems a simple and just conception that administrative costs and possible losses in disposal ought to be assessed against the product, so becoming a part of its direct costs rather than a government subsidy. Dissension over this feature of recent legislation is really ill-considered. Take away the fee and the whole cost must fall on the government to be paid for out of general tax funds. The real question, which needs much more exploration than it is getting, is whether the six billion dollars of annual loss to farmers ought to be taken from some other class and given to them. For this would be the intent of surplus-control legislation.

Opponents of farm relief talk as though a rise in farmers' incomes must necessarily come out of consumers' pockets. They arrive at this by admitting first that the exploitation of farmers helps to reduce urban living costs. Regardless of the justice of such an arrangement, a further exploration of the general economic situation into which a program of farm relief has to be injected, reveals a number of social costs in this which, if they were applied to the urban-rural balance sheet, might considerably reduce the advantages to urban consumers assumed to flow from farm depression.

Suppose, for the moment, that some governmental administrative device should succeed in raising the general farm income to a profitable level. This income will be spent. Its spending, either for capital goods or consumption goods, will enlarge factory production, provide more employment, probably reduce the per-unit costs of goods and possibly reduce prices. More employment and reduced prices are strictly equivalent to increased wages. Some unmeasured deduction from the supposed cost of farm relief must certainly be allowed for this series of events which would be consequent upon it.

The gross income of a nation cannot, of course, be increased by fiat. The assumption that factory production and urban employment will be increased by a shift of income from urban to rural folk rests on the further assumption that more is to be gained, at present, by the farmer's spending than by the spending of those who now receive income which is rightfully his. The low level of living and the inefficient methods of working in farm employments give distinct promise of this. There is, in other words, a more fertile field for the employment of higher incomes in rural life than in urban life. To a certain extent, therefore, deduction has to be made from the apparent cost of farm relief for the increase in the general income which might result from the employment of it in rural activities rather than in urban ones.

It ought also to be remembered that our present policy which involves a loss to farmers of, roughly, six billions a year, involves meeting the losses in some way or other. One way of meeting them is by land mining; another is by not depreciating equipment — barns, fences, machinery, stock; still another is by living on a restricted family budget — sacrificing health, education, morale. No person of sense would argue that these policies do not involve progressively higher costs for goods produced under the conditions they fix; and, ultimately, higher prices to their consumers. The temporary advantage of urban over rural folk may well turn out to be a costly one in the long run.

But if means were taken to correct this disadvantage a whole series of alternative events would be engendered. Increased farm profits would mean more capital equipment, better health and education, increased fertility, higher morale. These are the conditions under which the long-awaited technical reorganization of the industry might take place, with reduced costs of production and with lower prices to consumers.

Simple and arbitrary raising of farm prices will not produce these results. Limitation of production must be undertaken at the same time. Otherwise production will be extended to poor lands, operators will be encouraged in inefficiency, and we will be no better off than we are now. Many of the larger industries at the present time are so articulated as to be able to effect a limitation of their own production to profitable amounts. Farmers must buy their goods. But the nature of agriculture is such that no similar coördination is possible for farmers. The use of governmental machinery for such a purpose is not usual with us, but there would seem to be a quite reasonable excuse for it on these grounds.

One other feature of this cost problem is interesting. Regardless of whether we happen to feel that farmers' incomes ought to be made larger, they *will* be made larger, at least temporarily. For in every complete cyclical movement there is a period within which the advantage lies with farmers, when the index of farm prices rises above the price index of other commodities. Proposals for stabilization of the price relationship may sound slightly less horrific if this fact is kept prominent in the discussion. This period is shorter, less extreme, and therefore less profitable to farmers than the period during which their losses cumulate. But it nevertheless recurs. If it is argued that to raise farmers' incomes would upset the normal course of affairs, if it seems arbitrary and unjust to consumers of their products, these aspects of the situation are mitigated by remembering that, without intervention, all these things will, in time, occur. The plea is, in fact, more for order and regularity than for subsidy. And it may be germane to remark that this period of advantage for farmers seems to be a favorable one all round. They have gained most in prosperous times, with rising prices and widespread industrial activity. Their very inability, then, to change the supply of their products at less than a year's notice (more for many things: fruits, dairy products) is then a favorable circumstance, and their prices rise faster than those of other goods whose supplies are more readily enlarged. This cannot be expanded into a claim that increased farm prices result in prosperity. But it does throw some light on the question whether farm relief would necessarily be ruinous to other classes.

The ordinary "hard-boiled" type of person is fond of saying that if the farm problem is let alone the inefficient farmers will ruin themselves and those who can make money will eventually come to dominate the industry. There seems, however, to be considerable doubt as to whether the selection works this way. There are those who say that the efficient get out and the poor, because their shiftless standards content them, remain. And that, in consequence, the power of the industry to save itself is diminishing. In answer to citations of the undoubted fact that there are now, in every community, prosperous farmers, they say that these individual successes are only comparative, that they exist because the general technological level is so low, and that these examples cannot be cited as evidence of a probable salvation of the whole occupation from within.

It is true that successful farmers are to be found. But it is also true that they are prosperous because they produce a greater product with a given outlay of effort and capital. They can, because their costs are lower, accept prices which keep their more inefficient neighbors hopefully in business. But if efficiency should become the rule, as things are, the product of the farms would be increased enormously, and if there is anything in the surplus idea, prices might again tend to fall below costs of production. Efficiency would dig its own grave. This is because nothing would have happened to strengthen the farmer's general position as an economic unit among the others of our system. To supply this deficiency, coöperative marketing is suggested. Even President Coolidge approves this movement. It is conceived of as being the agricultural correlative of the corporation and the trade association in other businesses. And, actually, it has been given freer scope for development.

There is nothing wrong with this notion except that it does not seem to work very well. These possibilities have always existed; but the state of the industry at present is sufficient indication of their regenerative influence. Their failure to materialize is precisely the source of the reasoning which asks for governmental intervention, and which leads to the serious belief of many students that the industry must first of all be made prosperous. By this first step, and by a secondary regularization and limitation of activity the period of infancy may be shortened.

Limitation of production need not necessarily involve less food-products for the nation, or the wastage of land resources through abandonment. It may have quite opposite results. Staples, it is true, have a relatively inexpansible demand; but not all agricultural goods have, by any means, reached the limits of possible use. It is more true of those whose producers are now in most trouble; but limitation here would have general beneficial effects. We raise too much wheat for any purpose, probably; but the possible expansion of the use of dairy products — with lower prices — is very great, and this is true of numerous other products. Limitation of cotton, corn, wheat, and tobacco production would serve to stimulate others, enriching the whole economy. For not only would consumers be given wider and better choices, but farm practice would doubtless be improved by less emphasis upon a few crops and the expansion of others.

It is not generally remembered, in discussing farm relief, that we are now on the verge, probably, of a vast technological reconstruction of the industry. Ancient axioms, which have seemed almost native to the soil, are being called in question. The corn crop, for instance, the king of all American farm products, may very well disappear. Its cultivation contributes to erosion; it is costly to raise; it has new but formidable enemies, such as the borer. Alfalfa may take its place. The whole theory of rotation is under attack. It is rotation which offers the most formidable resistance to economical machine operation. These indicate a few of the many possible changes.

Up to now agricultural experts have preached variety and mixed farming in season and out. One-crop cultivation has been anathema. But because it lends itself to large-scale operations, and because land restoration no longer depends necessarily on animal humus, the one-crop system may very well increase rather than diminish.

So soon as we can see at all clearly what some of these new trends are likely to be, it will be a social duty to encourage them. A program of limitation entered on for temporary purposes now might later serve this purpose also. The long and short-run programs may interpenetrate one another. A general policy of limitation might involve expansion as well as repression. If the wheat crop were cut down, the alfalfa crop might be increased. In such a case both temporary and permanent gains would ensue. Then too we all must have read with wonder the new promises of the chemists. They think of the land and its vegetation as a sun-trap which now is mostly unused. They talk of billions of tons of unused raw stuffs and of a new alliance between agriculture and industry. Who shall say that nothing may come of it? And why might not the government supplement its program for agricultural planting with experimental manufacture, at least, of some of the things already made in laboratories from the waste products of the farms: rayon, wall-board, fire-proof tiles, synthetic lumber, insulators, and the like?

No program of limitation woud dare eliminate the possibility of surplus. The most troublesome surpluses indeed arise from the vagaries of nature. It would be necessary to provide machinery for protection against these risks. But here the McNary-Haugenites are correct. These risks are insurable. And only the government can undertake to spread the risks. The equalization fee is a device for doing it. It might be more pleasing constitutionally, to lay an excise tax on each unit to be insured, but the effect would be the same.

Given some assurance that insured profits would not yield an ever-increasing surplus from year to year, and there can be none but administrative objections to the McNary-Haugen Bill. The Bill of 1928 contained a half-effective answer to those who said that surpluses would increase. It was vaguely said that the Farm Board would advise farmers concerning planting programs, and that if the advice were not heeded the recalcitrant ones would be shut out from the benefits of profit-insurance. This may be as far as we can go with limitation. It may be far enough. I should like to have seen it tried as a beginning. Indeed the more I study the Bill of 1928 the deeper my admiration becomes. As a piece of social legislation it surpasses anything an American Congress ever framed. The remaining troublesome consideration is its dependence on a non-existent coöperative structure. Perhaps, however, ways around this difficulty may be found.

B. IMMIGRATION RESTRICTION

The Immigration Act of 1924 guided American policies until the nineteen sixties. There was little debate in Congress over the major restrictive features. It passed the House 326–71 and the Senate 62–9 with only a handful of legislators from urban centers opposed. In one important aspect, however, the version of the act approved by Congress defied the wishes of the Coolidge administration. Secretary of State Charles Evans Hughes and the President objected to the provisions excluding Japanese immigrants. Hughes contended that a treaty of 1911 had affirmed a "gentlemen's agreement" of 1907–1908 between the United States and Japan by which the latter consented to issue passports only to non-laborers or to laborers who came to the United States to join their families. West coast Congressmen, frightened by an increase in Japanese population, charged that the Japanese government was circumventing the agreement by issuing passports to "picture brides," and they contended, moreover, that the "gentlemen's agreement" was an executive infringement upon the legislative powers of Congress. Both houses decisively rejected the pleas of the President and the State Department and the final bill incorporated the Japanese exclusion clause.

Robert DeC. Ward, professor of Climatology at Harvard and a founder of the Immigration Restriction League in 1894, in describing and defending the act expresses the kind of racist thinking that underlay this unfortunate political legacy of the twenties decade.

ROBERT DEC. WARD

Our New Immigration Policy, *Foreign Affairs, III, September 1924,*
pp. 99–111

Reprinted by special permission from Foreign Affairs.
Copyright Council on Foreign Relations, Inc., New York.

On May 26, 1924, President Coolidge gave his approval to
what is officially known as the Immigration Act of 1924.
This new law marks a radical change in the immigration policy of the United States. Representative Albert Johnson, chairman of the Committee on Immigration and Naturalization of
the House of Representatives, has called it, without exaggeration, a second Declaration of Independence. (1) It establishes
a definite numerical limitation. (2) The bulk of immigration is
to be of the same racial stocks as those that originally settled
the United States and still constitute the major part of its
population. (3) There is to be a preliminary selection overseas.

This new policy of limitation and of selection, epoch-making
as it is, is all the more surprising when it is recalled that the
first general immigration act was passed as recently as 1882
and provided only for the exclusion of convicts (except in
the case of political offenses), of lunatics, of idiots, and of
persons likely to become a public charge. The Act of 1882
was amended and strengthened in various ways by later legislation, but even the last general immigration act, that of 1917,
which enumerated some thirty classes of aliens as subject to
exclusion for physical, mental, moral or economic reasons, involved no general limitation of numbers, no racial selection, and
no overseas inspection. The Chinese Exclusion Acts (1882 and
later), the "Gentlemen's Agreement" with Japan (1907), and
the so-called "Barred Zone" (1917) represented the only steps
which had been taken towards any serious policy of exclusion
or of numerical limitation, and all of these were concerned
only with people of Asiatic origin. Even the illiteracy test,
which was a storm-center of discussion for many years and
finally became a part of the Act of 1917, useful as it has

proved in several ways, has not operated appreciably to diminish numbers. The Quota Act of 1921, which limited new immigration to three percent of the number of foreign-born living in the United States at the time of the census of 1910, for the first time definitely restricted immigration as a whole, but was passed as temporary war emergency legislation and later extended (until June 30, 1924), still as a temporary measure.

When a nation as large and as powerful as the United States adopts a new policy on a matter of such importance, both to itself and to the rest of the world, it is pertinent to inquire into the causes. Let us therefore analyze, so far as may be possible, the general trend of public opinion on this subject, first in the period before federal control of immigration, and then in the three or four decades preceding the passage of the Act of 1924.

For a round hundred years it was a national ideal that the United States should be the asylum for the poor and the oppressed of every land. This very early came to be known as the "traditional" American attitude towards immigration. Curiously enough, there has always been a fundamental error in the popular conception of this tradition. This noble ideal of a refuge, open to all, had its roots in economic conditions far more than in any altruistic spirit of world philanthropy. For many decades the country was very sparsely settled. There was abundant free land. Labor was scarce. The number of immigrants was still very small, and nearly all of them were sturdy pioneers, essentially homogeneous and readily assimilated. There was, therefore, little need to worry about any immigration "problems," and it was comforting to the consciences of our ancestors to keep the doors wide open.

Gradually, in later years, as the stream of incoming aliens assumed what in those days were large proportions, and the first difficulties of assimilation began to appear, a second thought came into the national consciousness — that of the "Melting Pot." The fundamental idea in the theory of the Melting

Pot was that environment, not heredity, determines what human beings shall become. It was thought that the great American Melting Pot could fuse into a new homogeneous race, better and finer than the world had ever known, unlimited numbers of aliens of all nations, habits and languages who might choose to come here from any quarter of the globe. It was believed that sending alien children to school, teaching them English, giving them flag drills, letting them recite the Gettysburg Address and read the Declaration of Independence, would make thorough-going Americans of them, similar in all respects to the native-born of the traditional type.

While the dominant feeling for most of the period up to the end of the nineteenth century was indifferent to, or at any rate not in favor of, restrictive legislation, there were not lacking those who from the very foundation of the republic were opposed to free immigration. Washington questioned the advisability of immigration except of certain skilled mechanics. Jefferson expressed the wish that there were an ocean of fire between this country and Europe, so that it might be impossible for any more immigrants to come here. The Hartford Convention, in 1812, proclaimed that "the stock population of these states is amply sufficient to render this nation in due time sufficiently great and powerful."

When the influx of German and Irish assumed considerable proportions, the feeling against wholly unrestricted immigration grew rapidly, and many of the same arguments were then used as have become familiar in more recent years. It was urged that these people were of different race and religion, that they were undesirable competitors in the labor market, and that they presented difficulties of assimilation. The "Know-Nothing" agitation of the middle of the last century, which was largely anti-Catholic, for a time attained considerable political prominence but was not a restriction movement.

During the last decade of the nineteenth century a distinct change in public opinion began to manifest itself. Of slow growth at first, the new views soon spread more and more rapidly until they have finally been embodied in the new immigration law. Many persons have made the mistake of thinking that the war was the immediate and main cause of this change in the national immigration policy. To the present writer the situation appears in quite a different light. America's experiences during the war, and the prospect of what would happen as the war's aftermath, were unquestionably very potent factors in bringing about the new legislation, but a survey of the literature of immigration during the past thirty or forty years shows that throughout this period firm foundations were being laid upon which the public opinion of the country in favor of effective restriction was being built up. The reason for the gradual reversal of the earlier American policy of free immigration to one of steadily increasing restriction was the very marked change in the general character of immigration which began in the decade 1880–1890. It is significant that in the period 1871–1880 the "old" immigration from northern and western Europe amounted to slightly over 2,-000,000 persons while the "new" immigration, from southern and eastern Europe and near Asia, numbered only 180,000. In the years 1897–1914, the period immediately preceding the war, the "old" contributed about 3,000,000 while the "new" contributed over 10,000,000. The number of arriving aliens was increasing with enormous rapidity. Their racial origins and their characteristics were changing. It was at this point that a real and very serious immigration "problem" arose. The newer immigrants generally had different and lower standards of living. They often retained their loyalty to their native countries. They read their own foreign language newspapers. Barriers of every kind separated them from the native population and from earlier immigrants from northern and western Europe.

The seriousness of the situation was not immediately apparent to the great body of the American people. Most of the writers who dealt with it failed to grasp the importance of the change. But there were exceptions — men who labored to make plain the far-reaching racial, economic, politicial, and social consequences which would inevitably follow if a policy of unrestricted immigration were continued. In 1892 appeared the late Professor Richmond Mayo-Smith's "Emigration and Immigration," a pioneer volume in the new field. The late Prescott F. Hall clearly set forth the effects of the new immigration in his "Immigration" (1906), and urged the need of immediate and more adequate legislation. In 1894 a group of men in Boston organized the Immigration Restriction League, the first body of its kind in the country. This league has for thirty years been steadily at work, carrying on a general educational campaign for more effective restriction and selection. Americans began to realize that the ideal of furnishing an asylum for all the world's oppressed was coming into conflict with changed economic and social conditions. The cold facts were that the supply of public land was practically exhausted; that acute labor problems, aggravated by the influx of ignorant and unskilled aliens, had arisen; that the large cities were becoming congested with foreigners; that there were too many immigrants for proper assimilation; that large numbers of mentally and physically unfit, and of the economically undesirable, had come to the United States. Those who still honestly clung to the idea of maintaining in the United States a haven of refuge for the oppressed, one by one realized that America can only be such a haven if conditions here are better than they are in the lands from which our immigrants come, and that the only way to maintain our economic, political, educational, and social standards is by means of restriction.

The fallacies of the Melting Pot theory had also become obvious. [Years before the war it had become increasingly apparent that the Melting Pot was no longer successfully performing its function; that the American population was losing its homogeneous character; that various nationalities of recent immigrants were forming more and more compact racial "blocs," each bloc tenaciously maintaining its own racial character, customs, and traditions.] The United States was fast

increases
racism

we don't want to be a boarding house?

becoming, as Theodore Roosevelt expressed it, a "polyglot boarding house." Furthermore, Americans who gave attention to the results of biological investigation became cognizant of the fact that the laws which rule in the world of the lower animals are also dominant in the case of man. They realized that a heavy draughthorse cannot be made into a trotter by keeping him in a racing stable. Nor can a race true to the old American type be produced by any process of Americanization, so called. What goes into the Melting Pot determines what shall come out of it. If the material fed in is a varied assortment of nationalities, to a considerable extent physically and mentally below par, there can be no hope of producing a superior or even of maintaining a homogeneous race. It is often said, and with truth, that each of the different alien peoples coming to America has something to contribute to American civilization. But what America needs is desirable additions to, and not inferior substitutes for, what it already possesses. There is nothing in biological discovery or principles which would lead to the hope that only the virtues of the various races which were going to make up the future American would survive and the vices be eliminated. The public consciousness awakened to the realization that, to quote Dr. Henry Fairfield Osborn, "education and environment do not fundamentally alter racial values. . . . The true spirit of American democracy, that all men are born with equal rights and duties, has been confused with the political sophistry that all men are born with equal character and ability to govern themselves and others, and with the educational sophistry that education and environment will offset the handicap of ancestry."

In another important respect public opinion underwent a striking change in the decade or two before the war, namely in regard to the relation of immigration to the need for labor. So accustomed had Americans become to seeing vast numbers of foreign laborers flocking into the factories, and mills, and coal mines that it had come to be an axiom that the need for labor could only be supplied by a constant and unlimited inflow of immigration. From the time of the first agitation for restriction down to the present, large employers of "cheap labor" have always insisted that the development of industry and the prosperity of the country absolutely depend upon a free inflow of alien labor. Of late years, however, it has been seen that cheap foreign labor may often be so cheap that it is dear at any price; that it is usually, in the long run, both socially and politically very expensive; that a tremendously rapid development of the country is by no means altogether desirable. The conviction spread rapidly that, as Dr. H. H. Laughlin has clearly expressed it, "immigration is a long-time investment in family stocks rather than a short-time investment in productive labor." The question arose whether any American industry which cannot prosper without a continuous supply of cheap alien labor is really worth preserving in a country which boasts of the high standards of living of its wage earners and the high character of its citizenship. The feeling grew that a much more general use of labor-saving machinery, together with the natural increase of the present population, supplemented by a properly restricted and carefully selected immigration, would in time largely solve this labor problem. Americans are unalterably opposed to anything even approximating slave or coolie labor, of whatever race or color, in their country. It became evident that a continuance of the policy of unlimited immigration would inevitably produce here a permanent class of low-grade labor of the coolie type.

In line with this changing trend of public opinion on the question of cheap labor there has been noticeable recently a significant change of attitude on the part of certain far-seeing manufacturers, who realized that a permanent limitation of immigration was to be the settled future policy of the country and who began to adjust themselves to the new situation by decreasing their labor turnover and by increasing the use of labor-saving machinery. The attitude of this group has probably been correctly stated by Mr. Edward A. Filene of Boston, himself a large manufacturer and employer, as follows:

"Employers do not need an increased labor supply, since increased use of labor-saving machinery and elimination of waste in production and distribution will for many years reduce costs more rapidly than wages increase, and so prevent undue domination by labor."

Thus American public opinion had for twenty-five or thirty years before the war been gradually crystallizing in favor of more restriction. Abundant evidence of this tendency is to be found in the literature on immigration, as well as in the enactment of the successive laws of 1882, 1885, 1891, 1903, 1907, and 1917. The report of the United States Immigration Commission, completed in 1910, which recommended restriction "as demanded by economic, moral, and social considerations," was a very convincing official pronouncement on the question, and did much to convert the nation as a whole to the necessity of prompt action. This commission, it should be noted, suggested a percentage limitation of immigration.

Then came the Great War. Patriotic Americans who had been in doubt on the question of restriction became aggressive restrictionists. Those who had been advocating further effective legislation saw the tide turning their way with irresistible force. During the years of the war various alien racial groups in the country showed clearly enough that their sympathies were not American but European. European antagonisms, bred and nourished through the centuries abroad, came to the surface in the United States. Those who had been relying on the Melting Pot to accomplish assimilation realized that they had cherished false hopes. The statistics of the Draft threw a great deal of light upon the whole problem of the foreign-born in the United States. Americans suddenly awoke to a realization of the danger of having in their country an element of foreign birth, or with one or both parents foreign-born, which constituted one-third of the total population and of which a disquietingly large proportion were unfit for active service because of an inability to speak English or because of inferior intelligence. Further, competent authorities in the

United States and unprejudiced observers abroad united in the conviction that the war would be immediately followed by an immigration the volume of which would far exceed anything that had ever been known. Not only this. The new immigration would be composed almost wholly of eastern and southeastern Europeans: people of mixed races, with traditions, customs, political experience and standards of living radically different from those which had been the distinguishing characteristics of the American population. It was the verdict of observers abroad, both official and otherwise, that a Jewish mass-migration, more or less well organized, was imminent. It did not appear that such an immigration, composed chiefly of small shop-keepers, pedlers, and sweat-shop workers, would fill any real economic need in the United States. The lessons of the war, and the prospect of a vast immigration following it, suddenly fanned into a brighter flame the smouldering fire of sentiment in favor of restriction. The result was that in the Emergency Act of 1921 the United States for the first time placed a definite numerical limit on immigration.

With the three percent law expiring on June 30, 1924, Congress was faced with the necessity of providing adequate legislation to take the place of the Emergency Act. Under the able leadership of Representative Johnson, of Washington, and with the coöperation of the large majority of an unusually competent committee, an extraordinarly thorough study was made of every aspect of this complex subject. Numerous hearings were held, the published reports of which now constitute an indispensable part of the literature on immigration. In the Senate, Hon. David A. Reed, of Pennsylvania, had charge of the bill and showed great skill in dealing with the parliamentary situations there, as well as in suggesting an important amendment to the bill as it originally passed the House. The enormous majorities by which the bill passed Congress clearly reflected public opinion on this subject.

The main provisions of the Act of 1924 may, for the sake of simplicity and clearness, be grouped under three heads, (1) those dealing with limitation of numbers; (2) those providing for selection; (3) those based on humanitarian motives.

(1) *Limitation.* For three years, or until June 30, 1927, the annual quota is fixed at two percent of the number of foreign-born of each nationality in this country in 1890. This will admit, within the quota, somewhat over 160,000.[1] Under the emergency law of 1921, with its quota of three percent on the basis of the 1910 census, the countries of southern and eastern Europe, including Asiatic Turkey and Palestine, were given about forty-five percent of the total immigration, although they compose less than twelve percent of the total population of the United States. There was thus distinct discrimination in their favor, and no less distinct discrimination against the stocks which principally settled the American colonies and established the American form of government, and whose descendants make up over one-half of our white population today. The quotas, in other words, were based on the number of foreign-born in the United States, and took no account of the Americans born in America. The percentage provision in the new law, based on the census of 1890, gives these same countries of southern and eastern Europe and near-Asia quotas roughly in the same proportion to the total immigration as the persons born in those countries and now in the United States bear to the present population of the United States. Southern and eastern Europe will now have slightly over fifteen percent of the total quota immigration — a liberal

---

[1] It is to be noted, however, that immigrants who were born in the Dominion of Canada, Newfoundland, Mexico, Cuba, Haiti, the Dominican Republic, the Canal Zone, or an independent country of Central or South America, and their wives and unmarried children under eighteen if accompanying or following to join them, are allowed to come in without limitation as to numbers provided they are admissible under the provisions of the general immigration act of 1917, which still remains in force as to the classes of aliens who are subject to exclusion for certain physical, mental, economic or moral reasons. Experience in the operation of the new law may show that this very liberal exception in favor of the countries of the Western Hemisphere will require limitation.

allowance in view of the fact that they constitute slightly less than twelve percent of the total population. "The use of the 1890 census is not discriminatory. It is used in an effort to preserve as nearly as possible the racial *status quo* in the United States. It is hoped to guarantee, as best we can at this late date, racial homogeneity in the United States."[2]

There was no question of the racial superiority of northwestern Europeans or of the racial inferiority of southeastern Europeans. It was simply a question as to which of these two groups of aliens is, as a whole, best fitted by tradition, political background, customs, education, and habits of thought to adjust itself to American institutions and to American social and economic conditions — to become, in short, an adaptable, homogeneous and helpful element in American national life.

Sec. II (b), of the Immigration Act of 1924 reads as follows: "The annual quota of any nationality for the fiscal year beginning July 1, 1927, and for each fiscal year thereafter, shall be a number which bears the same ratio to 150,000 as the number of inhabitants in continental United States in 1920 having that national origin bears to the number of inhabitants in continental United States in 1920, but the minimum quota of any nationality shall be 100." This is Senator Reed's racial origins provision. It cuts straight through the controversy as to whether the quotas should be based on the census of 1890 or that of 1910. It bases the quotas not upon the numbers of those composing the various alien colonies or foreign "blocs" now in the country, ignoring the native-born, but divides them among the nationalities in accordance with the national origins of the whole population. The fairness of such an apportionment cannot be disputed. It declares, in effect, that what we now are racially we propose to remain. Against such a stand there can be no ground for opposition. Each year's immigration, as Commissioner Curran put it, is to be "an exact miniature of what we are as to stock." This is bedrock immigration

---

[2] 68th Congress, 1st Session, H. R. Report No. 350.

policy. It is one of the fairest and most constructive provisions which has ever been embodied in any immigration law.

The so-called Japanese exclusion clause of the Act of 1924 was the subject of more discussion than any other part of the measure. Apart from its diplomatic aspects, it has far more importance as the establishment of a principle than as a means of limiting immigration. With certain fairly numerous and reasonable exceptions, it excludes aliens ineligible to citizenship, thus covering all Orientals. Since 1907 the limitation of Japanese immigration had been accomplished, not by law enacted by Congress, but by an understanding with Japan known as the "Gentlemen's Agreement," which was neither treaty nor law. The insistent demand for the exclusion of Orientals, and the determination of Congress to regulate immigration itself by law, combined to bring about the inclusion of the "ineligible to citizenship" provision in the new legislation. This law settles it once for all that immigration is a domestic matter which Congress proposes absolutely to control and that it is not a subject for treaty.

(2) *Selection.* Another important feature of the new law is the attempt, for the first time, to exercise some control over immigration at the source. Intending immigrants must apply to United States consular officers abroad for "immigration visas." These papers are to contain answers to questions essentially the same as those asked the immigrant on his arrival at our ports, together with full information as to the alien's family status, his occupation, personal appearance, ability to speak, read and write, addresses of relations, destination, personal and family institutional history, etc. In addition, the alien must furnish, if available, copies of his "dossier" and prison and military record, and copies of all other available public records concerning him kept by the government to which he owes allegiance. "The application is to be signed by the alien in the presence of the consular officer, and verified by oath administered by that officer. No immigration visa is to be issued if it appears to the consular officer, from statements in

the application or in the papers submitted therewith, that the immigrant is inadmissible to the United States under the immigration laws," nor "if the consular officer knows or has reason to believe that the immigrant is inadmissible to the United States under the immigration laws." Visas for quota immigrants are to be issued only up to the numbers allowed by the quotas, and are to be good for a period not exceeding four months. This plan of visas does not constitute medical or general inspection overseas. That inspection is to be carried out, as it always should be, in the United States, by American inspectors, American doctors, and where American hospitals are provided. But the new plan will at least accomplish a preliminary selection overseas. While there will undoubtedly be many cases of perjury and of fraud in this connection, there can be no question that a great many undesirable aliens, subject to exclusion by law, will be refused their papers by our consuls when application is made.

The new plan is the first real attempt on the part of the United States to exercise some control over the kind of immigrants who shall come here. Hitherto this matter has been left practically altogether in the hands of foreign countries, some of which have certainly had no hesitation about making it easy for their own least desirable citizens to come to America.

(3) *Humanitarian provisions.* The new law contains many provisions based on broad humanitarian motives. The immigration visa plan should reduce hardships to a minimum, prevent the division of families, and put an end to deportations on account of arrivals in excess of the quotas. Congestion at Ellis Island, with its attendant hardships, will be done away with, and it will therefore be possible to make the medical and general examinations more thorough and more effective. Further, "an immigrant who is the unmarried child under eighteen years of age, or the wife, of a citizen of the United States who resides therein at the time of filing a petition" is admissible as a "non-quota" immigrant provided there is no medical or other ground for exclusion; and in the issuance of immigration

visas preference, up to fifty percent of the annual quota of any nationality, is to be given to an alien "who is the unmarried child under twenty-one years of age, the father, the mother, the husband, or the wife, of a citizen of the United States who is twenty-one years of age or over." These two provisions should surely be sufficiently liberal in preventing the separation of families. Indeed, experience may show that these exceptions in favor of near blood relatives are too liberal, and are open to abuse, in which case they can be modified by law. Among the humanitarian sections mention may further be made of the permission to reënter the United States after temporary absence, and the admission, as non-quota immigrants, of ministers, professors (including their wives and unmarried children under eighteen), and *bona fide* students.

Further, more effective provision is made for preventing the embarkation of aliens who fall into the excluded classes by increasing the fines on the transportation companies in cases where such aliens are brought to the United States. If intending immigrants of this sort are kept from sailing, hardship and suffering are very greatly reduced. Heavy fines on the transportation companies are the only means by which the United States can prevent these companies from taking the passage money from aliens who may later be deported. In each case the Secretary of Labor is to satisfy himself, before imposing the fine, that the existence of the disease or disability might have been detected by competent examination, medical or otherwise, or by "reasonable precaution" at the time of foreign embarkation. In addition, the steamship company is to refund to the alien the price of his ticket from his initial point of departure to the port of arrival. All these provisions are distinctly humane, and in the interests of the alien as well as of the United States.

In all, it can truthfully be said in regard to the Act of 1924 that no immigration measure has had such careful drafting and such diligent, humane and disinterested consideration. It is an emphatic national decision that, to quote President

Coolidge, "America must be kept American." It is based on bedrock principles. It marks a turning point in American civilization.

PRESENT IMMIGRATION QUOTAS

Provided by Act of Congress,[3] approved March 26, 1924, and proclaimed by President Coolidge June 30, 1924

(For each of the countries indicated by an asterisk is established a nominal quota according to the minimum fixed by law. These nominal quotas, as in the case of all quotas hereby established, are available only for persons born within the respective countries who are eligible to citizenship in the United States and admissible under the immigration laws of the United States.)

Country	Quota	Country	Quota
*Afghanistan	100	Great Britain and Northern	
Albania	100	Ireland	34,007
Andorra	100	Greece	100
Arabian peninsula	100	Hungary	473
Armenia	124	Iceland	100
Australia	121	*India	100
Austria	785	Iraq (Mesopotamia)	100
Belgium	512	Irish Free State	28,567
*Bhutan	100	Italy (incl. Dodekanesia,	
Bulgaria	100	etc.)	3,845
Cameroon (French)	100	Japan	100
Cameroon (British)	100	Latvia	142
*China	100	Liberia	100
Czechoslovakia	3,073	Liechtenstein	100
Danzig, Free City of	228	Lithuania	344
Denmark	2,789	Luxemburg	100
Egypt	100	Monaco	100
Esthonia	124	Morocco	100
Ethiopia (Abyssinia)	100	*Muscat (Oman)	100
Finland	471	Nauru	100
France	3,954	*Nepal	100
Germany	51,227	Netherlands	1,648

[3] "The annual quota of any nationality shall be two per centum of the number of foreign-born individuals of such nationality resident in continental United States as determined by the United States census of 1890, but the minimum quota of any nationality shall be 100" — Sec. 11(a). "For the purposes of this Act nationality shall be determined by country of birth" — Sec. 12(a).

PRESENT IMMIGRATION QUOTAS (Continued)

Country	Quota	Country	Quota
New Zealand	100	*Siam	100
Norway	6,453	South Africa, Union of	100
*New Guinea, etc.	100	South West Africa	100
Palestine	100	Spain	131
Persia	100	Sweden	9,561
Poland	5,982	Switzerland	2,081
Portugal	503	Syria and The Lebanon	100
Ruanda, Urundi	100	Tanganyika	100
Rumania	603	Togoland (British)	100
Russia, European and		Togoland (French)	100
Asiatic	2,248	Turkey	100
Samoa, Western	100	*Yap, etc.	100
San Marino	100	Yugoslavia	671

C. PRIVATE OR PUBLIC CONTROL OF MUSCLE SHOALS?

The controversy over the disposition of the nitrate plant built by the government during the war at Muscle Shoals, Alabama, masked more serious issues. In an era when electricity increasingly ran the nation's factories and lighted its homes, the power industry assumed an importance in the economy like only to that of the railroads a generation earlier. How was this great new industry to be regulated? Would private or public interests control the vital generating facilities on the nation's waterways? In the long debate over Muscle Shoals, Senator George Norris of Nebraska never lost sight of the broader issues involved. In his autobiography he describes the tortuous political path from the Muscle Shoals debates to the authorization of the Tennessee Valley Authority.

GEORGE NORRIS
Fighting Liberal
New York: The Macmillan Company, 1945, pp. 249–267

For whatever inspiration and encouragement it may be to the American people in their struggle against well-intrenched, enormously rich, and powerful forces, and the selfishness, confusion, and misunderstanding they inject, this "log" of some of the successive steps in the struggle for TVA furnishes some slight knowledge of the battle:

1921: Secretary of War Weeks asked for bids for the leasing of Muscle Shoals. The thought was private development and operation.

July 8, 1921: Henry Ford first submitted his bid. Committee hearings opened.

February 6, 1922: S.J. 159, for acceptance of Ford offer, introduced in Senate with committee support, together with other bills of a similar character.

December 5, 1923: House bill to dispose of properties to Ford again introduced; passed both House and Senate, but with amendments, and finally died through lack of action on conference committee report.

January 5, 1926: S.J. Res. 2147 introduced by Norris to provide for the operation of Dam No. 2 at Muscle Shoals, for the contruction of other dams on the Tennessee River and its tributaries, and for the incorporation of the Federal Power Corporation. Referred to committee; no action taken.

December 15, 1927: S.J. Res. 46 by Norris providing for the completion of Dam No. 2 at Muscle Shoals and the steam plant at Nitrate Plant No. 2 for the manufacture and distribution of fertilizer and for other purposes. This passed both houses of Congress but received pocket veto by President Coolidge in June of 1928.

May 28, 1929: S.J. Res. 49 by Norris "to provide for the national defense by the creation of a corporation for the operation of the government properties at or near Muscle Shoals and for other purposes." It passed both branches of Congress and was vetoed by President Hoover, and the veto sustained March 3, 1931.

December 9, 1931: S.J. Res. 15 by Norris "to provide for the national defense by the creation of a corporation for the operation of government property at or near Muscle Shoals." No action taken.

April 11, 1933: S.J. 1272 by Norris "to improve the navigability and to provide for flood control of the Tennessee River, provide for reforestation and the proper use of marginal land in the Tennessee valley; to provide for the agricultural and industrial development of the valley; to provide for the national defense by the creation of a corporation for the operation of government property at or near Muscle Shoals, and for other purposes." In lieu of this, H.R. 5081 passed House, after introduction by Congressman Lister Hill, and Norris moved to take up the House bill, strike out all after the enacting clause, and substitute the Senate bill, which was done.

There, in most abbreviated form, are the milestones marking the legislative struggle over the Tennessee Valley Authority. There were many other resolutions and bills to turn Muscle Shoals to private interests in the opening phases of the fight.

It was a most natural opposition to the entire principle of TVA that developed in the beginning.

I was certain a majority of the members of Congress in both branches were against development of Muscle Shoals by the federal government.

If for no other reason than the conservative tendencies of those years, expressed on every street corner and throughout the rural regions, there was raised a nearly insurmountable barrier to TVA. Private enterprise, it was said, had built America. Its initiative, its energy, its genius, and its great vision had made the American people strong, sturdy, rich — the best fed and the best cared-for people in the world. Congress accepted that doctrine generally without reservations, gladly and honestly. People believed it. There was the proof in the young and vigorous nation, which had outstripped its older rivals, and enjoyed infinitely more comforts and luxuries than other nations. Governmental operation and ownership was looked upon with great suspicion, distaste and open resentment.

It was by accident, the result of America's participation in World War No. 1, that the national government on its own initiative had taken the first, uncertain step for a development of this magnitude on a national scale. That war emergency was the chief reason, among many, why the Tennessee valley was selected as the proper site, or the testing ground, for this national movement.

War had made the question of nitrates a very critical and exceedingly important consideration. They were needed in all kinds of military operations, and for the production of explosives. To a very great extent, the United States, as well as other nations of the world, had been depending upon nitrates which came from Chile. Immediately submarine warfare, coupled with the sinking of ships by "surface raiders," raised a question of transportation of these nitrates from South America to the American mainland where they could be conserved properly, and utilized later to supply the American fighting forces with the necessary explosives to carry on and to win the war.

Nitrogen in its natural state was one of the most plentiful of all the ingredients which go into explosives.

It was in the air all around and about in inexhaustible quantities.

But to extract nitrogen from the air under the methods then prevailing required a vast amount of electricity. It could not be produced economically without fabulous amounts of cheap power. In Norway, a nation blessed with swift, deep streams, lending themselves admirably to the development of cheap power and cheap electricity, one process for producing nitrogen had been in existence for a number of years.

Another, more effective and economical method, known as the cyanamide process, had been developed; but it too required a very great amount of electricity.

This was the emergency which led the federal government to undertake the development of cheap power by proper conservation on some of the streams of the United States. Congress had authorized the President, Woodrow Wilson, to select locations for such developments, and Mr. Wilson, upon recommendations by the engineering counsel, chose Muscle Shoals and began construction of Wilson Dam.

The intention was to make the United States independent of the necessity of importing nitrates from South America.

There also had been the hope that development at Muscle Shoals would result in the production of a cheaper form of commercial fertilizer for worn-out land as a permanent, valuable aid to agriculture. The two objectives fitted into each other. Through Muscle Shoals it was hoped to obtain adequate nitrogen for the explosives needed in war, and later for fertilizer in time of peace. A cheaper fertilizer would be a great boon to the older regions of the United States, making possible abundant crops, and an improvement in the status of farm families who were existing miserably on soil whose fertility had been depleted.

It was recognized that completion of Wilson Dam would take considerable time and was no overnight job.

As a short cut from dependence upon foreign nitrogen, it was determined to construct a steam plant at Muscle Shoals to supply the electric power for the production of nitrates while the war lasted. The steam plant was built, in a much shorter time than Wilson Dam, and the nitrate plant itself required much less time for construction. It became known as Nitrate Plant No. 2, built by the American Cyanamid Company under the supervision of the government, while work was being pushed rapidly on Wilson Dam.

It was known also Germany must have perfected some other process for the production of nitrates. That rigid blockade maintained by the vigilance of the navies of the Allied nations hemmed Germany in, and made it impossible for her to obtain Chilean nitrate. While American chemists and scientists were not sure of the secret methods employed by Germany, they thought they had uncovered them. So a pilot plant, known as nitrate plant No. 1, and a second steam plant to provide the electricity which would be needed by it, were built near by, largely as an experiment.

This pilot nitrate plant naturally was not as large as its prede-cessor; and although it was completed it never was put into production. All the expenditures upon it, together with the outlay for a second steam plant, were lost. Never a pound of nitrate came from these developments, but the desperate con-dition which existed fully justified the attempts. There could be no complaint because of futile expenditures, under the cir-cumstances, the necessity of producing nitrates constituted a national emergency. The cyanamide process adopted in Nitrate Plant No. 2 meant production was very costly — perhaps too costly to supply a cheap fertilizer in times of peace.

Before Wilson Dam was finished, war was over.

Then the scientific world learned of the process used by Ger-many in extracting nitrogen from the atmosphere, and thus carrying on the struggle even though the Allied blockade had cut her off from the South American source of supply.

The German method, known as the Haber process, was a very material improvement over the cyanamide formula and was much less costly.

Immediately private corporations in this country rushed to construct plants utilizing the Haber process.

It was then that it fell to Congress to determine the future of Muscle Shoals. It was then that the proposal for bids from private corporations received much public approval; it was then Mr. Ford made his offer and the congressional conflict began. Numbers of resolutions were offered to turn Wilson Dam over to private owners. There was the Underwood bill later, which in itself precipitated a bitter fight, and under the provisions of which the resources of the Tennessee valley would have fallen into private hands represented by a number of associated private corporations.

Of all the measures to turn over the resources of the Ten-nessee River to private development, I think that that of Henry Ford had more popular support than any other. A distinguished American, he is one of America's wealthiest and most successful men. He had captivated American imagination. He had produced a cheap automobile, established the most satisfactory relationships with the workers in his factories, and demonstrated he was a man of great vision, daring, and dreams. About that time the industrial giants of America had become the nation's heroes.

It was on July 8, 1921, that Henry Ford submitted his proposal for the leasing of Muscle Shoals. Nearly a year passed before House hearings were completed; and out of the hearings H.R. 11903 emerged in the House of Representatives, providing for acceptance of the Ford offer. There were other bills providing for the acceptance of Mr. Ford's offer, and for leasing Muscle Shoals to other interested groups. At the same session and subsequent sessions, there were resolutions and bills calling for new congressional surveys and for establishing commissions to complete studies. It was a period of great confusion and uncertainty of purpose in Congress.

Not until the opening days of December in 1923, did friendly sentiment towards acceptance of the Ford offer crystallize in the House and the Senate to bring about passage of H.R. 518, which was a duplicate of the Ford bill of the year before.

With many amendments added in the Senate, the measure went to conference; and agreement upon the differences was finally reached by the conferees in a report to both houses on February 6, 1925. It was a "Lame Duck" session of Congress, and adjournment was due in six days, so that no action was taken on the conference report by either branch of Congress.

Muscle Shoals occupied the same status after four years.

I fought all these bills.

In the main, the senators representing the southern states were in favor of accepting Mr. Ford's proposal.

After studying it, and the entire subject, to the best of my ability, I had reached the unalterable conclusion I could not support any proposition turning all of this property over to Mr. Ford. I had become convinced that every bill which had been introduced contained provisions which made it impossible for the plan to succeed. I argued at that time the cyanamide process of getting nitrogen from the atmosphere was too expensive to be of practical benefit in the production of cheap fertilizer for agriculture — the emergency of war, with the immediate need of nitrates for explosives, having passed.

I have no way of knowing how this blistering controversy, which Mr. Ford's offer had inspired in the Senate, would have ended had not he, himself, withdrawn the offer.

This withdrawal did not end it.

Still the fight between private interests on one side and government ownership and operation of Muscle Shoals on the other was far from settled. There was a very considerable sentiment remaining expressed in the Underwood bill, but I noted and took hope in the weakening of opposition. There were other aspects in which personal profit played a very large and agonizing part. The expectation that Mr. Ford or some other individual or group would obtain Muscle Shoals, upon which the government had expended millions, and would operate it for private gain and profit, ushered in an era of active real estate speculation in sections of the Tennessee valley. Thousands of honest men and women were led to invest their savings in real estate in the belief they were getting in on the ground floor of a new American wonderland.

I know Mr. Ford had no knowledge these real estate manipulations were going on.

*   *   *

With withdrawal of Mr. Ford's offer, the struggle over Muscle Shoals simplified itself to an issue between those who believed in public ownership and development of the power at Muscle Shoals and throughout the entire Tennessee valley, and the "power trust," seeking to prevent anything of the kind.

The private power companies never offered to develop the stream which it desired to prevent the government from touching.

Power, in reality, was not the first consideration of the Tennessee Valley Authority in any bill that I introduced in Congress over a period of years. Power was not even the most important of the considerations.

I, at least, always have believed that the first and most important objective was the control of the flood waters of a great river, which in turn affected the Ohio from the mouth of the Tennessee to the mouth of the Ohio, and the Mississippi from the mouth of the Ohio to the Gulf of Mexico.

All the years I was in Congress until completion of the Tennessee Valley Authority, frightfully destructive floods had rolled down the tributaries of Tennessee from their headwaters in the Alleghenies, in gathering volume to inflict great damage upon property and human life along the Tennessee, the Ohio, and finally the Mississippi.

In the months that followed these floods, there was not enough water left in the Tennessee to maintain navigation.

The bills which I introduced provided, without exception, for maintaining navigation on the Tennessee from Knoxville to the mouth in Kentucky, where it empties into the Ohio. They called for a normal channel, with a nine-foot flow of water. To accomplish it, flood waters had to be held back in the reservoirs and released during the seasons of low stream flow.

In this way, and only in this way, the destruction resulting from floods could be eliminated, or reduced to a minimum.

Up to this point, the fight had been much more confused.

Mr. Ford's offer, supported perhaps by a majority of the Senate, with nation-wide attention favorably focused upon it, had been clear, plain, and understandable to the people.

By contrast, I had no specific plan, and I realized all along my position did not present a practical method of utilizing all the power developed by the steam plant and the even greater electrical energy to be supplied by Wilson Dam.

I think I had demonstrated beyond argument that nitrogen from the atmosphere could be obtained much more cheaply by scrapping Nitrate Plant No. 2 and constructing an entirely new one embodying the Haber process.

That in itself had involved long study.

The Du Pont company (either a subsidiary or the parent corporation of the gigantic organization) had constructed a nitrogen plant near Charleston, West Virginia, utilizing the German Haber process for extracting nitrogen from the air.

I determined upon a personal examination of that plant at Charleston, and requested the War Department to assign to me one of its representatives who, while not a chemist, had had partial control of the construction of Nitrate Plant No. 2 at Muscle Shoals.

Secretary Weeks agreed to my request, and the examination was made.

The Du Ponts sent their principal chemist, a most generous and thoughtful aid, to meet me. He proceeded to make everything accessible to us; no objection was placed in the path of any investigation I desired to make. From what I saw, it became clear to me a new plant for Muscle Shoals could be constructed for much less money than the original one had cost, operated at much less expense, and would produce much more nitrogen.

Still the position I occupied was a very difficult one.

There was always the argument that since Uncle Sam had expended so many millions in the construction of this cyanamide plant, it should be utilized either under the Ford proposal or under some other, such as may have been contemplated in the Underwood bill.

There was only one answer.

I think I demonstrated before the Agricultural Committee of the Senate, through the testimony of the most eminent chemists and scientists, the cyanamide process never would be a success. New discoveries and new processes had antiquated its methods, although they were all right in their day.

And now the controversy was broadening infinitely.

It was my consistent argument that the construction of these reservoirs along the tributaries and on the Tennessee would prevent all damage from floods in the Tennessee valley and lessen the destruction on the Ohio and the Mississippi. The Tennessee, I pleaded, could be made navigable the year around. No longer was power the sole objective, or even the chief purpose.

If floods were controlled successfully, it followed naturally that erosion could be prevented to a very great extent. Already the winds whipping against the hillsides, the rains beating down, the floods churning through its valleys, had carried away into the river itself much of the fertile soil of the Tennessee region, with the result that the lands had lost some of their productivity and had become much less valuable for agricultural purposes.

The silt carried into the streams interfered seriously with navigation.

I thought I could look ahead to a time when thousands of people would be compelled either to abandon the land entirely, or to live in the utmost squalor and poverty.

If these flood waters were controlled by the construction of high dams to hold back the flow in reservoirs, necessarily it followed that, by the expenditure of comparatively small additional sums, electrical power could be generated at the dams as a by-product and distributed freely to the people of the entire region at prices much lower than they had been compelled to pay.

It was this which brought the irreconcilable, embittered, and uncompromising enemy — the power trust — into the fight.

It had no fundamental objection to making the Tennessee River navigable, but in pursuance of its own interest it preferred an unnavigable river to any interference with its monopolistic control of the generation and sale of electric power. For a long time it had claimed that the way to improve the Tennessee River, or any other stream, was to build low navigation dams at much less cost than the dams which I advocated; and in this plan it said the river would be navigable even in low water.

It was an argument which would not stand analysis.

Navigation, to be practicable, must be as unimpeded as possible.

Ships passing through fifty, sixty, or more low navigation dams would be confronted with impossible impediments. The great reservoirs, some of them located on the river itself, some on the tributaries, by the use of the high dam, would expedite navigation through sets of locks. Vessels would be elevated from a lower level to a higher level through the locks and they could sail for miles without impediment over artificial lakes, speeding up navigation, making it practical, and making it profitable.

At the same time these artificial lakes and high dams would produce electricity, all of which would be lost by the construction of only low navigation dams.

One high dam could make the river navigable for many miles and eliminate the necessity of constructing scores of low navigation dams.

*   *   *

In the closing stages of this fight, all the forces that could be mobilized against the Tennessee Valley Authority were drawn in.

There were the coal companies.

Their opposition was inspired by an argument that labor in the coal mines would be the loser if TVA developed the vast amount of power that was contemplated. The figures have shown that the coal companies have not come into competition with TVA activities but actually have made more money and have sold more coal since TVA than they sold before.

The truth is that electric power is rapidly becoming a necessity in every modern community, but until recent years the prices for it have been so high that its full use has been denied to millions of people.

I remember the case of John L. Lewis.

Mr. Lewis always had been opposed to the TVA Act —
honestly, no doubt, believing that the generation of vast
amounts of electric power would deprive many of his miners
of their jobs. The TVA purchases and uses a large amount of
coal; has constructed and built several generating plants where
coal is used exclusively for the generation of power. Mr.
Lewis' attitude simply demonstrated that any man who stands
in the way of human progress and seeks to prevent the use of
technological improvements is standing in his own way and
blocking his own progress.

Not only has TVA brought reduced prices to the firesides
in the homes where electricity is consumed; but it has improved
agricultural conditions in the great Tennessee valley beyond
all hopes and expectations of those who favored the TVA
legislation. This was inherently a part of the struggle for final
congressional approval of the bill I introduced at the opening
of each session of Congress.

At the end of seven years' fight, following months of congressional battle, TVA passed both branches in June of 1928;
but President Coolidge killed it by pocket veto. Again, two
years later Congress passed TVA; but President Herbert
Hoover sent my hopes crashing to the lowest point they
reached in all those years when he vetoed it in a sharp message
assailing the principles of government ownership and operation.

I tried unsuccessfully to override the veto.

The power trust with all the vast resources at its command,
utilizing fully every ounce of influence it could wield in a last-
ditch fight, naturally had sought to create the impression that
nothing more was concerned in the TVA program than the
generation of electricity through harnessing the streams under
a program of public ownership and operation.

The truth was that power was only a by-product — important because it would contribute most to the recovery of the
necessary outlays of public funds to carry out all of the objectives of the TVA. This I repeated session after session until

TVA passed Congress for the third time in April of 1933 and was signed by President Roosevelt.

D. SECRETARY OF TREASURY MELLON'S TAX REDUCTION PLAN

The wartime Revenue Act of 1918 had raised taxes to the highest point in the nation's history. Taxable incomes up to $4000 were assessed at 6%; those over $4000 at 12%. The total tax in the highest income brackets could run as high as 77%. In addition the federal government collected an excess profits tax and a series of luxury taxes.

In 1921, 1923, and again in 1926, Secretary Andrew W. Mellon presented to Congress a comprehensive plan for reducing these taxes. Most controversial was his proposal to slash the maximum surtax from the wartime peak of 77% down to 25%.

Although Mellon's proposals had the strong backing of Presidents Harding and Coolidge, Progressives and Democrats in Congress seriously amended the tax reduction plan both in 1921 and 1923. For example, the Revenue Act of 1921 as finally approved, repealed the excess profits tax but cut maximum rates only to 50% beginning in 1922. The Revenue Act of 1924 reduced normal tax rates much in the pattern Mellon requested, but cut the maximum surtax only to 40%, not 25%.

The Secretary won a decisive victory in 1926 when the Democrats in Congress reversed themselves and demanded even more stringent cuts in taxes and more severe budget reductions than the parsimonious Republican administration. The maximum surtax was set at 20%; all that Mellon did not achieve was repeal of the federal estate levy.

In the first selection that follows, Secretary Mellon outlines and defends his 1923 proposal. In the second, the *New Republic* in a 1926 editorial appraises the significance of the Mellon victory both for the backsliding Democrats and the triumphant Republicans.

ANDREW W. MELLON
Taxation: The People's Business
New York: The Macmillan Company, 1924, Appendix A, pp. 175–189.
Reprinted with permission of the publisher. Copyright 1924 by the
Macmillan Company, renewed 1952 by Nora McMullen Mellon.

[*Letter from the Secretary of the Treasury to the Acting Chairman of the Committee on Ways and Means, November 10, 1923.*]

In accordance with the request which you made shortly after the adjournment of Congress, the Treasury has been engaged for the past few months in considering the possibilities of tax revision and in developing recommendations for the simplification of the law. The situation has developed more favorably than was anticipated, and I am now presenting to you a comprehensive program to which I hope the Committee on Ways and Means will be able to give consideration at the outset of the legislative session.

The fiscal years 1922 and 1923 have each closed with a surplus of about $310,000,000 over and above all expenditures chargeable against ordinary receipts, including the sinking fund and other similar retirements of the debt. This has been possible only through the utmost cooperation between the Executive and Congress, as well as among the executive departments and establishments, all of whom have united in a sincere effort to reduce the expenditures of the Government. At the same time there has been a substantial amount of realization upon securities and other assets remaining over from the war, and the Treasury has succeeded in collecting customs and internal revenue taxes in amounts somewhat exceeding original expectations. The result is that the Government of the United States is firmly established on the basis of having balanced its budget each year since the cessation of hostilities, with a reasonable surplus each year after providing for fixed debt charges like the sinking fund, and stands squarely committed to the policy of including these fixed charges on account of the public debt in its ordinary budget each year, thus assuring an orderly reduction of the war debt out of current revenues.

What has been done during the two years since the establishment of the budget system shows clearly what united effort can accomplish, and gives every reason for hope that the task to which the Administration has set itself for this fiscal year can be successfully performed, namely, the reduction of the ordinary expenditures of the Government to a total of not more than $3,500,000,000, of which about $500,000,000 will be fixed charges on account of the sinking fund and other retirements of the debt. To do this means reductions of about $170,000,000 in the estimates of expenditures submitted by the spending departments and establishments and the exercise of continued pressure all along the line for the utmost economy and efficiency in the operations of the Government.

Having these things in mind, the Treasury has been canvassing the estimates for the present fiscal year and for the succeeding fiscal years with a view to determining on the one hand what further reductions in expenditure it would be safe to count on in developing a tax-revision program, and on the other hand what receipts might reasonably be expected on the basis of existing law, assuming that no changes were to be made in internal taxes. In doing this it has had to keep in mind that under present conditions receipts from customs are abnormally high and that surplus war supplies have now been for the most part liquidated, leaving relatively little to expect on this account in the years to come. It has also had to keep in mind that many of the internal revenue taxes, as, for example, the higher brackets of the surtax, are so rapidly becoming unproductive that it is unsafe to assume that even with no changes in the law the revenues from internal taxes would be maintained. After taking into account all these considerations, and making the most conservative estimates about the yield of existing taxes and the possibilities of further reductions in expenditure, it appears that for this year, and for the next four or five years, there should be a surplus of something over $300,000,000 a year over and above all expenditures chargeable to the ordinary budget, including the fixed debt charges payable out of current revenues. This gives a reasonable margin not merely for tax revision but also for tax reduction.

On this basis the Treasury has the following recommendations to make:

1. *Make a 25 per cent reduction in the tax on earned income.* The fairness of taxing more lightly income from wages, salaries and professional services than the income from a business or from investment is beyond question. In the first case, the income is uncertain and limited in duration; sickness or death destroys it and old age diminishes it. In the other, the source of the income continues; it may be disposed of during a man's life and it descends to his heirs. It is estimated that this amendment will mean a loss in revenue of about $97,500,000 a year, the greater part of which falls in the lower income brackets.

2. *Where the present normal tax is 4 per cent reduce it to 3 per cent, and where the present normal tax is 8 per cent reduce it to 6 per cent.* This affects all personal incomes and the loss of revenue comes largely from the lower brackets. It is estimated that this will mean a loss in revenue of $91,600,000 a year.

3. *Reduce the surtax rates by commencing their application at $10,000 instead of $6,000, and scaling them progressively upwards to 25 per cent at $100,000.* This will readjust the surtax rates all along the line, and the Treasury recommends the readjustment not in order to reduce the revenues but as a means of saving the productivity of the surtaxes. In the long run it will mean higher rather

than lower revenues from the surtaxes. At the outset it may involve a temporary loss in revenue, but the Government Actuary estimates that even during the first year, if the revision is made early enough, the net loss in revenue from all the changes in the surtaxes would be only about $100,000,000, and that in all probability the revenue from the reduced rates will soon equal or exceed what would accrue at the present rates, because of the encouragement which the changes will give to productive business.

The readjustment of the surtaxes, moreover, is not in any sense a partisan measure. It has been recommended, on substantially this basis, by every Secretary of the Treasury since the end of the war, irrespective of party. The present system is a failure. It was an emergency measure, adopted under the pressure of war necessity and not to be counted upon as a permanent part of our revenue structure. For a short period the surtaxes yielded much revenue, but their productivity has been constantly shrinking and the Treasury's experience shows that the high rates now in effect are progressively becoming less productive of revenue. See Table II, hereto attached. The high rates put pressure on taxpayers to reduce their taxable income, tend to destroy individual initiative and enterprise, and seriously impede the development of productive business. Taxpayers subject to the higher rates can not afford, for example, to invest in American railroads or industries or embark upon new enterprises in the face of taxes that will take 50 per cent or more of any return that may be realized. These taxpayers are withdrawing their capital from productive business and investing it instead in tax-exempt securities and adopting other lawful methods of avoiding the realization of taxable income. The result is to stop business transactions that would normally go through, and to discourage men of wealth from taking the risks which are incidental to the development of new business. Ways will always be found to avoid taxes so destructive in their nature, and the only way to save the situation is to put the taxes on a reasonable basis that will permit business to go on and industry to develop. This, I believe, the readjustment herein recommended will accomplish, and it will not only produce larger revenues but at the same time establish industry and trade on a healthier basis throughout the country. The alternative is a gradual breakdown in the system, and a perversion of industry that stifles our progress as a nation.

The growth of tax-exempt securities, which has resulted directly from the high rates of surtax, is at the same time encouraging extravagance and reckless expenditure on the part of local authorities. These State and local securities will ultimately have to be paid, principal and interest, out of taxes, thus contributing directly to the heavy local taxation which bears so hard on the farmers and small property owners. There is no immediate remedy for this within the power of Congress except the readjustment of the surtaxes on a basis that will permit capital to seek productive employment and keep it from exhausting itself in tax-exempt securities. The productive use of capital in our railroads and industries will also tend to bring lower costs for transportation and manufactured products, thus helping to relieve the farmer from the maladjustment from which he now suffers.

4. *Limit the deduction of capital losses to 12½ per cent of the loss.* The present revenue law limits the tax on capital gains to 12½ per cent but puts no limit on the capital losses. It is believed it would be sounder taxation policy generally not to recognize either capital gain or capital loss for purposes of income tax. This is the policy adopted in practically all other countries having income tax laws, but it has not been the policy in the United States. In all probability, more revenue has been lost to the Government by permitting the deduction of capital losses than has been realized by including capital gains as income.

So long, however, as our law recognizes capital gains and capital losses for income tax purposes, gain and loss should be placed upon the same basis, and the provisions of the 1921 Act taxing capital gains at 12½ per cent should be extended to capital losses, so that the amount by which the tax may be reduced by the capital loss will not exceed 12½ per cent of the loss. It is estimated that this will increase the revenues by about $25,000,000.

5. *Limit the deductions from gross income for interest paid during the year and for losses not of a business character to the amount the sum of these items exceeds tax-exempt income of the taxpayer.* The 1921 Act provides that interest on indebtedness to acquire or carry tax-exempt securities is not deductible. This provision is ineffective because a taxpayer may purchase tax-exempt securities for cash and borrow money for other purposes. It is felt also that so long as a taxpayer has income which is not reached for taxation, he should not be permitted to deduct his non-business losses from the income which is taxable, but should be restricted in the first instance to a deduction of these losses from his non-taxable income. The estimated increase of revenue from this source is $35,000,000.

6. *Tax community property income to the spouse having control of the income.*

So much for the income tax recommendations, which should became effective January 1, 1924. In order that you may have before you a clear view of the effect of these recommendations as applied to incomes in the various brackets, I am attaching a table, prepared by the Government Actuary, showing the estimated results of the proposed changes in the calendar year 1925, on the basis of the taxable year 1924. The schedule shows a loss of revenue of about $92,000,000 in the brackets under $6,000, and a further loss of revenue of about $52,000,000 in the next bracket of $6,000 to $10,000. In short, about 70 per cent of the reduction would be in the brackets of $10,000 or less, and less than 5 per cent would fall in the brackets over $100,000.

To show the effect of the proposed changes on the income of a typical salaried taxpayer, married and having two children, I call your attention to the following comparative figures:

Income	Present tax	Proposed tax	Saving to taxpayer
$4,000	$28.00	$15.75	$12.25
5,000	68.00	38.25	29.75
6,000	128.00	72.00	56.00
7,000	186.00	99.00	87.00
8,000	276.00	144.00	132.00
9,000	366.00	189.00	177.00
10,000	456.00	234.00	222.00

7. *Repeal the tax on telegrams, telephones and leased wires.* . . .

8. *Repeal the tax on [movie] admissions.* . . .

9. *Miscellaneous nuisance taxes.* Your Committee may wish to consider the elimination of various small miscellaneous taxes which have an inconsiderable bearing on the general revenue of the Government, but which are a source of inconvenience to taxpayers and difficult to collect. . . .

10. In addition to the specific recommendations which directly affect Government revenues, there should be amendments to strengthen the Act and eliminate methods heretofore used by taxpayers to avoid imposition of the tax. The exact amount of additional revenue to the Government which will be brought in by these amendments cannot be estimated, but certainly the amendments will reach much income that heretofore has escaped taxation.

11. *Establish a Board of Tax Appeals in the Treasury*

*but independent of the Bureau of Internal Revenue, to
hear and determine cases involving the assessment of internal revenue taxes....*

In order that you may see the effect on Government
revenues of the above recommendations, I submit the following figures as to the estimated result of these changes:

	Decrease (in millions of dollars)	Increase (in millions of dollars)
Reduction of 25% in tax on earned income	97	..
Reduction in normal tax	92	..
Readjustment of surtax rates	102	..
Capital loss limited to 12½%	..	25
Interest and capital loss deductions limited	..	35
Community property amendment	..	8
Repeal of telegraph and telephone tax	30	..
Repeal of admissions tax	70	..
TOTAL	391	68
	68	
NET LOSS	323	

The benefits of the reduction will be distributed among
all classes of taxpayers, and the revision generally will help
to free business and industry of vexatious interference
and encourage in all lines a more healthy development of
productive enterprise.

The present burden of taxation is heavy. The revenues
of the Government are sufficient to justify substantial reductions and the people of the country should receive the
benefits. No program, however, is feasible if the Government is to be committed to new and extraordinary expenditures. The recommendations for tax reduction set
forth in this letter are only possible if the Government
keeps within the program of expenditure which the Bureau of the Budget has laid down at the direction of the
President. New or enlarged expenditures would quickly

eat up the margin of revenue which now appears to be available for reducing the burden of taxation, and to embark on any soldiers' bonus such as was considered in the last Congress or any other program calling for similarly large expenditure would make it necessary to drop all consideration of tax reduction and consider instead ways and means for providing additional revenue. A soldiers' bonus would postpone tax reduction not for one but for many years to come.[1] It would mean an increase rather than a decrease in taxes, for in the long run it could be paid only out of moneys collected by the Government from the people in the form of taxes. Throughout its consideration of the problem the Treasury has proceeded on the theory that the country would prefer a substantial reduction of taxation to the increased taxes that would necessarily follow from a soldiers' bonus, and I have faith to believe that it is justified in that understanding. Certainly there is nothing better calculated to promote the well-being and happiness of the whole country than a measure that will lift, in some degree, the burden of taxation that now weighs so heavily on all.

The Victory of Mellonism, *New Republic, 45, February 17, 1926, pp. 343–344*

The early votes on the disputed clauses of the new tax bill, such as those which reduce the super-taxes and revoke the provision for publicity, indicate what the final result will be. After having been defeated twice in his attempt to do away with the exceptionally heavy taxation of huge incomes, Mr. Mellon has finally won a complete victory. Hereafter the

---

[1] A Veteran's "adjusted compensation" (bonus) bill had passed Congress in 1922 but was vetoed by President Harding. A similar measure was enacted over the veto of President Coolidge in 1924.

United States government will not collect more than 20 percent from any taxpayer, no matter if he receives $10,000,000 a year. It will levy 20 percent on all incomes above $100,000. It will apply, that is, the principle of gradation upon moderate incomes up to $100,000, but renounce its application for the benefit of the very rich. Those who are responsible for this tenderness to multi-millionaires justify it on the ground that taxation at a higher rate than 20 percent is unproductive, but in the Senate bill they also abandon the only tax which the federal government could use to reach fortunes which are invested in tax-exempt securities or have by any other means escaped the super-taxes. They do away with the federal estate tax. This particular example of tenderness to the very rich will probably be revoked in part, for the House of Representatives is reported to be in favor of retaining some measure of federal inheritance taxation, but the existing rates will be reduced and the way will be prepared for its ultimate discard. Finally, the government will also abandon the principle that an income tax return is a matter of public record which should be accessible to other people besides its maker and the tax officials. As a result of these lower schedules the war debt will not be reduced as rapidly as it has been and its burden will to an increasing extent be passed on to future generations. In every practicable way the present Congress will "reform" the system of federal taxation in order to suit the convenience and promote the power of a few thousand owners of very large fortunes.

The new tax bill is the natural sequel to the election of President Coolidge by an overwhelming majority. The administration believes frankly and sincerely in this policy, and so do all but a small minority of the Republican party. Nevertheless the policy is not being carried into effect by virtue of Republican votes. On the two previous occasions when Mr. Mellon attempted to relieve the rich of the burden of super-taxes, he was defeated in the Senate by a combination between the Democrats and the progressives. If the Democrats had persisted in their former opposition, he would probably have been defeated by a similar combination on this occasion. His victory is traceable chiefly to an alliance between the two major parties. In this respect, as we have frequently pointed out, the Democrats have reversed their recent policy, repudiated the traditions of their party in respect to taxation, and permitted themselves to behave as the accomplices of the most extreme and characteristic brand of Republicanism. The Democrats are apparently disintegrating as an organized political group. The nomination of John W. Davis by the last Democratic national convention after the battle between McAdoo and Smith was the preliminary symptom of this disintegration. It was the first indication that the several factions could not muster the energy to differ radically from the Republicans without differing more radically from one another. At present the Democracy can unite only on a neutral policy or a neutral candidate.

Deserted by the Democrats the progressives are not unnaturally discouraged by the poor showing which they are making in the present Congress. Ever since 1910 progressive policies have at different times obtained a large measure of support in both parties, whereas now they are rejected by both parties, and the progressive representatives in the House and Senate are reduced to a mere handful. Of course it *is* discouraging to the members of a once powerful group to find themselves comparatively without influence in the government of their country, but they should not take their present impotence too seriously. If the progressives are justified in believing that a plutocratic government cannot in the long run promote the welfare of the American people, they can count with confidence on the future revival of resistance to the Republican party. Its policy is bound to stimulate popular expectations and needs which its government cannot continue to satisfy. It will provide a fertile soil for abuses which its

leaders will not have the courage to remedy. When progressivism does revive, the Democrats will be unable to capi-
talize it for their own benefit. They have disqualified themselves for dealing radically with the economic issue. Bryanism
as a formative influence in the Democracy is dead. It died
during the presidential campaign of 1924 while Bryan himself
was still alive.

The disintegration of the Democracy will improve the
chances of Republican success at the next one or even two
elections, but in the end it will create a vacuum which will
have to be filled by a more vigorous and capable opponent.
It will, that is, offer to the progressives an opportunity of
dominating the formation of a party which will resist Republicanism instead of serving as its accomplice. That is why the
progressives should not be discouraged by the refusal of the
Democrats to coöperate with them in fighting Mellonism,
but should as a result of this backsliding regard their prospects
with increasing confidence. The government of the country
by two parties, both of which were partly and occasionally
progressive and partly and occasionally the reverse, has for
a generation served to smother American progressivism. If
one of these parties is by way of disintegrating, a new party
alignment is foreshadowed in which progressivism should
count as a positive factor.

It will not, of course, form the only positive factor. The
New Republic has frequently called attention to the increasingly sharp definition of a cultural conflict between the older
puritan small-town, native-born, Nordic Americanism and the
newer easy-going Americanism of foreign origin which is
growing up in the large cities. This conflict is at the present
moment an effective agent of Democratic disintegration. It
is, indeed, directly responsible for the extinction of Bryanism
in the Democratic party, and indirectly responsible for the
recent refusal of the Democrats in Congress to share with the
progressives the fight against Mellonism. The Smith faction in
the Democratic party considered it necessary to declare war

on Bryanism in its economic as well as its Ku Klux aspect. It will doubtless continue to underemphasize the economic issue as long as its immediate objective is that of ruling or ruining the Democratic party. But after it has broken with the old Democracy for the purpose of asserting the cultural interests of the increasing urban population, it will be obliged in order to obtain recruits from other classes and justify its independent existence to take a sharp issue with Republicanism; and it cannot fight Republicanism without joining the progressives in fighting Mellonism.

During the next few years the position of the Republican party will have become extremely vulnerable. The temporary weakness of its opponents will increase its self-confidence and the disposition of its rich beneficiaries to profit from their privileges and opportunities. They will be far too powerful and successful for their own deserts. They will be too exclusively responsible for success in keeping the Coolidge Utopia alive. As soon as prosperity diminishes, the economic machine begins to creak and abuses are exposed, they will have to assume the whole burden of popular suspicion and resentment. They will have done nothing to anticipate the reaction and prepare against it.

Party Stalemate and Political Indifference

CHAPTER 4

What little enthusiasm the campaign of 1926 engendered centered in contests for state offices and prohibition referenda. When the ballots had been counted, the Republicans had lost 22 seats in the House and 6 in the Senate leaving the party distribution in the upper house at 46 Republicans, 47 Democrats and one Farmer-Laborite.

The Nation promptly interpreted the results as a slap in the face to President Coolidge; what little hope the editors could muster for the future of American politics rested on the fact that Progressives in the Senate now held a balance of power.

Walter Lippmann in one of the most perceptive political commentaries of the decade, "The Causes of Political Indifference Today," raised more provocative questions. Given Coolidge prosperity, a benevolent "new capitalism" that anesthetized against the old Progressive grievances, and given the fact there were "no parties, no issues, no leaders," indifference was to be expected. "Current conservatism and progressivism," Lippmann contended, "are irrelevant." The most important political issue of the twenties, the one that stirred emotional crusades like prohibition and anti-evolution laws, was the rapid growth of the cities at the expense of the countryside. This metamorphosis was already reshaping the Democratic party and, Lippmann prophetically argued, a realignment within the confident Republican party lay not too many years in the future.

Mr. Coolidge, the Election, and the Future, *The Nation*, *123,*
November 17, 1926, p. 498

So Mr. Coolidge believes that he and his Administration
were not defeated at the polls. At least that is the assurance
he gave to the correspondents three days after the election.
He had lost control of the Senate? Yes, but you see that had
to do only with personal and local issues. The only national
part of the election related to the House of Representatives,
and there his party kept control albeit his majority sank from
59 to 37 and the latter figure counts the eleven insurgent Congressmen from Wisconsin as Republicans. So the President
rests in peace and is not even troubled by the fact that his own
State administered an overwhelming defeat to Senator Butler,
his Man Friday, his national chairman, his sponsor, and his
chief supporter in Massachusetts.

Now we do not deny that there was no single compelling
national issue in this election and that the several Senatorial
contests did hinge upon such matters as the corruption in Indiana, Illinois, and Pennsylvania, the dry-Republican bolt from
Wadsworth in New York, and other questions. But in his
own State Mr. Coolidge himself made the issue perfectly clear;
he demanded the return of Senator Butler, whereas in all other
States he refused to interfere in the contests. He went to his
old home to vote for the Senator, and he allowed that gentleman to make his whole campaign upon the necessity of supporting the President. Mr. Coolidge himself wrote that Senator Butler's presence in the Senate "is of great importance to
me in my efforts to discharge the duties of my office," and
he assured his State that in the Senate Mr. Butler "holds a
place which no one else could command for Massachusetts,
admired for his wisdom, respected for his integrity"! Among
the many Republican spellbinders who came from outside of
Massachusetts, Colonel Theodore Roosevelt the Lesser asserted
that the defeat of Butler would be a slap in the President's face.

Whereupon the electorate rose in its might and slapped Mr. Coolidge's face with a Walsh majority of 54,955. Yet Massachusetts is normally Republican and Mr. Coolidge is supposedly its favorite son. The Butler campaign began more than a year ago and was fortified by unlimited money and the support of some of the most influential dailies — and Butler was defeated. If this was not a direct and personal rebuke for the President, what in the world could be?

Again, disguise it as Mr. Coolidge will, the loss of control of the Senate is still another blow to the Administration. It is idle to assert that the President is happy to have a divided Congress. Negative as his personality and policies are, Mr. Coolidge knows that he will be largely judged in 1928 by his achievements during the next two years. That is already proved by his sudden proposal to return to the income taxpayers next year as a rebate their final income-tax payment of 1926 — a move hailed in both Republican and Democratic camps as entirely political. But the President cannot stop there. To what else will he "point with pride" in June, 1928? More than that, the control of the Senate has passed to men who are far more dangerous to him and to his policies than the Democrats, who are the merest shadow of an opposition, wholly without constructive leadership. The balance of power now rests with the group of Republican Progressives who, together with Senator Shipstead, the Farmer-Labor Senator, constitute the hope of political progress today. Norris, La Follette, Nye, Frazer, and Shipstead are now reinforced by Brookhart of Iowa and Blaine of Wisconsin, with whom will stand at times, on varying issues, Borah, Couzens, and Howell, Republicans, and Wheeler and Dill, Democrats. It is with them that the President will have to reckon. . . .

What use will the Progressive Senators make of their power? If we can appeal to them it is in the direction of urging them to unite upon a program and to map out a consistent policy for the next two years. They must themselves be the opposition the country so sorely needs. It is they who must focus the spotlight of publicity upon the White House and reveal its pretenses and its shams. It is they who can now draw for the public, the public which has administered his first defeat to the President, the true portrait of Calvin Coolidge. If they are wise they will do their utmost to prevent the President's renomination for a third term. This Massachusetts election, which has removed from the Senate one of the most harmful of our reactionaries, should set men's tongues free in other camps also. The fear of the President's power and patronage may now pass. If so, that will be one of the greatest benefits of the election. We are, of course, not so optimistic or inexperienced as to believe that we shall make great progress during the next two years. But the removal of men like Butler, and Ernst, and Wadsworth, the militarist, from Washington is clear gain, and the strategic position of the Progressives a promise of vigorous stirring in what would otherwise be an utterly arid political desert.

WALTER LIPPMANN

The Causes of Political Indifference Today, *The Atlantic Monthly*, *139, February 1927, pp. 261–268*

The record shows that in the last campaign President Coolidge appealed twice to the voters. Once he asked them to vote, to go to the polls and vote, to mark ballots for somebody. And once he emerged from behind the veil of the official spokesman's unofficial and indirect discourse to plead with the people of Massachusetts for his friend and campaign manager, Senator Butler. This attitude was a fair example of how the country felt about the election. A voter ought to vote. That was generally admitted in theory. But in practice the private citizen, like the President of the United States, was interested only in some one local election. . . .

Nobody was very much interested in the nation. Investigation would show, I am told, that the Republican National Committee was never called into action during the campaign, and that most of its energies since 1924 have been devoted to celebrating the personal virtues of Mr. Coolidge and to repairing the deficiencies of Senator Butler in Massachusetts. Its component factions engaged in a series of local elections from which not only Mr. Coolidge, but the national organization as well, held aloof. The party as a national organ abdicated, and either the voter had to follow Mr. Coolidge's example and excite himself about a local issue or he had not to excite himself at all.

The principles of the Democratic Party were likewise determined by geography. This party, too, had no national policy whatever. It too conducted a series of local campaigns, which were not only independent one of the other, but contradictory. . . . The only difference between the Republicans and the Democrats was that the Republicans were split apart and didn't know it, whereas the Democrats were split apart and knew it. They could not help knowing it after the convention of 1924 in Madison Square Garden.

In fact, as one contemplates the activities of politicians there is little doubt that, if only there were voters somewhere who wanted it, Republican and Democratic principles could be accommodated locally to polygamy, foot binding, or voodooism. The rule is simply this: anything which helps you to carry your state is the immortal principle of Abraham Lincoln and Thomas Jefferson.

It is not surprising, then, that national partisan politics should have come to mean so little to the ordinary voter. There are no parties, there are no leaders, there are no issues. There are parties only in the states, there are leaders only of sections, there are issues, but they are either evaded by national public men or carefully confined to the localities. There is nobody in American public life to-day who, like Roosevelt or Wilson is really a leader in all parts of the country. Mr. Coolidge has enjoyed popularity and confidence for two years, but the record of his leadership of Congress shows that he is essentially the representative of the Eastern tariff-protected interests. Neither Western agriculture nor the Eastern exporting interests have ever laid much of a hold on his mind. Mr. Lowden, undoubtedly the most powerful figure in the background of Republican politics, is devoting himself wholly to that agricultural interest which Mr. Coolidge has ignored. Senator Borah has touched almost every question and has come to grips with none; with all his great promise and immense personal opportunity he has failed to transform an attractive provincial insurgency into any sort of coherent national policy. . . . On the Democratic side there is Governor Smith, idol of the urban Democrats of the Northeast, but as yet wholly unknown, untried, and unexpressed on national questions. There is Governor Ritchie in Maryland, who may fairly claim to have a set of Democratic national principles, but who has not as yet a Democratic national following. And there is Senator Reed of Missouri, who has at least got this far nationally: he has made himself a holy terror to Republicans and Democrats alike.

The effect of these political disharmonies is to bewilder the electorate and to make the voters feel that politics is an elaborate game which has no serious and immediate consequences. This bewilderment manifests itself as complacency or as cynicism. Since 1920 the country has witnessed brazen and expensive corruption. In the amount of money involved the corruption is without parallel in our history. In its sordidness it is surely as bad as and probably a little worse than the scandals of the Grant administration. . . . In their public speech public men have been as complacent as possible about it all, and privately they have been prepared to explain that 'Well — oh well, you know, politics is a dirty game.' Maybe it is. But only a few years ago the country was still naïve enough, was still sentimental enough, to have become violently indignant over a cabinet officer accused of bribery. Indignation of this sort we have not known during these last few years. That too perhaps helps to explain why the interest in politics is at such low ebb, and why voting is not looked upon as such a very high duty. The impression has gone out from the White House that there is no use caring too much whether public officials are honest or whether elections are bought.

This persistent dampening down of popular interest in popular government has been the calculated policy of Mr. Coolidge ever since he became President. The reason given for it is that nothing must be done to distract business. The other reason for it, not given, but perfectly well understood, is that it is good politics when you are in power to discourage all manifestations of discontent. Mr. Coolidge is not exactly an ardent spirit. He is contented with little things; he is hardly suited to large thoughts and large deeds. He has not attempted them. On the contrary he has devoted himself to encouraging the people to turn their eyes away from the government. In peaceful, prosperous times not much encouragement is needed. Public spirit is at best a fragile thing when it comes into competition with the urgent demands of our private lives for money, for power, and for pleasure. So it has not been difficult for Mr. Coolidge to persuade the country that it need not take a vivid interest in public affairs.

Yet neither the personality of Mr. Coolidge nor the very special political strategy which he adopted will by itself account for the lethargy of spirit which has prevailed during his administration. Under different circumstances the virtues of Mr. Coolidge would almost certainly have been looked upon as vices. Mr. Coolidge has been praised for failing to lead Congress, for failing to lead his party, for refusing to become indignant at abuses, for not having a positive policy and a constructive programme. He would not have received this praise had the country not been in the mood for a negative administration.

It is the fashion to explain this mood by saying that after all the tall talk heard under Roosevelt and Wilson the country was exhausted emotionally and needed a rest. It had had its fill of idealism, of prophecy, of adventure, and of public action. It needed to forget Washington and the White House and the President, and tend to its private affairs. There is something in this explanation, of course, as there is also in the theory that the war brought a deep disenchantment with politicians, policies, and with what used to be called 'progressivism.' But all these explanations are obviously incomplete. For when you have said that men were tired of public affairs you have still to explain why, being tired of public affairs, they are able to indulge themselves by neglecting public affairs.

With this question we come, I think, nearer to the root of the matter. The American people, since the industrial recovery of 1922, has enjoyed an amazing prosperity. Except here and there in a few spots there has been such a surplus of wealth that practically the whole people has raised its standard of life. It was obvious that the opportunities to make money were so ample that it was a waste of time to think about politics. Nothing a man could hope to gain by voting for politicians, and by agitating for laws, was likely to be half so profitable as what he could make by participating in the boom.

The interested motives which are the driving force of political agitation were diverted to direct profit making. Now progressivism, as we have known it in the past, has arisen out of the belief of the debtors, the employees, the consumers, the farmers, that they could by changing the laws obtain a larger share of the national income. With the stupendous surplus available these last years, it has seemed to most men quicker and easier to go out and make money than to work through the cumbersome indirect processes of political action. Thus there has been no political discontent, except in a few farming states where the new surplus of wealth was not available, and where in consequence the old progressive motives and traditions survived. The common people looked to Roosevelt and to Wilson (before 1914) for relief from poverty and economic servitude. They did not look to Mr. Coolidge for relief because they were finding it by themselves. I am not attempting to say, of course, how real or how permanent is this relief; the fact which counts is that from about 1922 on almost everybody has had the feeling that he had a lot of money in his pocket, and would soon have more. It was this feeling which robbed progressive idealism of its urgency, and made it appear abstract and unimportant.

Together with this diffused prosperity, I should set down as a fundamental cause of political indifference the rise of what may be called the New Capitalism. There is no doubt that the large corporations are now under the control of a very different kind of man than they were when Roosevelt and Bryan and La Follette were on the warpath. The new executive has learned a great deal that his predecessor would have thought was tommyrot. His attitude toward labor, toward the public, toward his customers and his stockholders, is different. His behavior is different. His manner is different. His press agents are different. I am far from thinking he is perfect even now, but I am certain that he is vastly more enlightened and that he will take ever so much more trouble to please. He is no doubt as powerful as he ever was, but his bearing is less autocratic. He does not arouse the old antagonism, the old bitter-end fury, the old feeling that he has to be clubbed into a sense of public responsibility. He will listen to an argument where formerly he was deaf to an agitation.

Whatever may be the intrinsic good and evil of such things as the wide distribution of securities, however questionable may be some of the practices . . . the net result of the new attitude on the part of capital has been to create a new attitude on the part of the public. The press agents of the corporations have been told to woo the public, and their wooing has been successful. Suspicion has died down. Yet here again we must recognize that it would not have died down if capitalism as we know it were not making most people feel quite comfortably well off. During the last four years the actual prosperity of the people, combined with the greater enlightenment of the industrial leaders, has removed from politics all serious economic causes of agitation. There has been no pressing reason for an alignment of 'haves' and 'have nots,' and no reader of history needs to be told that when you remove economic discontent you remove what is certainly the greatest cause, if it is not the mainspring, of political activity. Politics carried on for justice, for liberty, for prestige, is never more than the affair of a minority. For the great majority of men political ideals are almost always based upon and inspired by some kind of economic necessity and ambition.

These circumstances account for the striking differences between European and American politics. The European finance ministers have had to struggle with deficits, ours with a surplus; they have had to impose taxes, ours to reduce taxes. The European nations have had to borrow, we to lend; they to devise means of payment, we to find ways of receiving payments. They have had to struggle to raise a low standard of living, and we to protect a high standard. They have had to reconstruct and restore; we have had only to perfect and expand. To Europeans, therefore, the American situation has seemed almost idyllic, and there has appeared a great literature in Europe which discusses the American economic system, often with admiration, sometimes with envy, always with the implication that it is one of the most extraordinary phenomena in history. Here in the United States during the last few years capitalism has worked in a way which confounds those who, like most educated Europeans, were brought up to think of it according to the socialistic formula, as an industrial system destined soon to be superseded by some kind of collectivism. Events have taken a wholly unexpected turn in the United States, and the advanced thinker here and abroad suddenly finds that he is no longer advanced. His descriptions, his analyses, his programmes, all assume a different course of evolution. The more or less unconscious and unplanned activities of business men are for once more novel, more daring, and in a sense more revolutionary, than the theories of the progressives. Action has moved faster than thought in these last few years, and practice is ahead of the programmes.

This lag in the development of theory has had a curious effect on political discussion. Public speakers, if they are conservative, will usually be found defending practices that their supposed clients are rapidly abandoning; if they are progressive, they will be found rather wearily and half-heartedly repeating the charges and the idealisms that were current a decade ago. The real industrial development of the day, with its momentous social consequences, hardly figures at all in public discussion. The philosophy of it is not yet understood; we have not yet learned how to talk about it. The good and the evil it contains have not yet been registered and assayed. And as a result most public controversy seems not so much like hot air as stale air. Without knowing just why, most of us feel, I think, that the *current conservatism and progressivism are irrelevant*. They do not satisfy our minds or grip our emotions.

The questions which really engage the emotions of the masses of the people are of a quite different order. They manifest themselves in the controversies over prohibition, the Ku Klux Klan, Romanism, Fundamentalism, immigration. These, rather than the tariff, taxation, credit, and corporate control, are the issues which divide the American people. These are the issues men care about. They are just beneath the surface of political discussion. In theory they are not supposed to be issues. The party platforms and the official pronouncements deal with them obliquely, if at all. But they are the issues men talk about privately, and they are, above all, the issues about which men have deep personal feelings.

These questions are diverse, but they all arise out of the same general circumstances. They arise out of the great migration of the last fifty years, out of the growth of cities, and out of the spread of that rationalism and the deepening of that breach with tradition which invariably accompany the development of a metropolitan civilization. Prohibition, the Ku Klux Klan, Fundamentalism, and *xenophobia* are an extreme but authentic expression of the politics, the social outlook, and the religion of the older American village civilization making its last stand against what looks to it like an alien invasion. The alien invasion is in fact the new America produced by the growth and the prosperity of America.

The evil which the old-fashioned preachers ascribe to the Pope, to Babylon, to atheists, and to the Devil is simply the new urban civilization, with its irresistible economic and scientific and mass power. The Pope, the Devil, jazz, the bootleggers, are a mythology which expresses symbolically the impact of a vast and dreaded social change. The change is real enough. The language in which it is discussed is preposterous only as all mythology is preposterous if you accept it literally. The mythology of the Ku Klux Klan is a kind of primitive science, an animistic and dramatized projection of the fears of a large section of our people who have yet to accommodate themselves to the strange new social order which has arisen in their midst.

This new social order is dominated by metropolitan cities of which New York is the largest and most highly developed. Therefore New York has become the symbol of all that is most wicked and of all that is most alluring in modern America. But New York to-day is only what Chicago, St. Louis, Detroit, Cleveland, Jacksonville, and Miami expect to be to-morrow. It is the seat of a vast population, mixed in its origins, uncertain of its social status, rather vague about the moral code. In these metropolitan centres the ancient social bonds are loosened. The patriarchal family, the well-established social hierarchy, the old

roots of belief, and the grooves of custom are all obscured by
new human relationships based on a certain kind of personal
independence, on individual experiment and adventure, which
are yet somehow deeply controlled by fads and fashions and
great mass movements.

The campaign in certain localities to forbid the teaching of
'Darwinism' is an attempt to stem the tide of the metropolitan
spirit, to erect a spiritual tariff against an alien rationalism
which threatens to dissolve the mores of the village civilization.
To many of us the effort seems quixotic, as indeed it is, judged
by the intellectual standards of metropolitan life. But if we
look at the matter objectively, disregarding the petty manner-
isms of the movement, there is a pathos about it which always
adheres to the last struggle of an authentic type of human living. The anti-evolutionists are usually less charming than Don
Quixote. Perhaps that is because they have not been trans-
figured by an artist. They are at any rate fighting for the
memory of a civilization which in its own heyday, and by its
own criteria, was as valid as any other.

The anti-evolution bills are, of course, a comparatively trivial
symptom of this profound maladjustment. The overt struggle
turns politically on two questions: on the Eighteenth Amendment and on the nomination of Governor Alfred E. Smith.
The struggle over these two issues implicates all the antagonisms between the older America and the new. The Eighteenth
Amendment is a piece of legislation embodied in the Constitution which attempts to impose the moral ideals of the villages
upon the whole nation. The force behind the Eighteenth
Amendment is the Anti-Saloon League, which is the political
arm of the evangelical churches in the small communities. The
financial and political strength of the Anti-Saloon League is
derived from the members of these churches, chiefly Methodist and Baptist, with other denominations divided but following these militant sects. And the strength of these sects in
the last analysis arises from the spiritual isolation of communi-

ties which have not yet been radically invaded by the metropolitan spirit.

The defense of the Eighteenth Amendment has, therefore, become much more than a mere question of regulating the liquor traffic. It involves a test of strength between social orders, and when that test is concluded, and if, as seems probable, the Amendment breaks down, the fall will bring down with it the dominion of the older civilization. The Eighteenth Amendment is the rock on which the evangelical church militant is founded, and with it are involved a whole way of life and an ancient tradition. The overcoming of the Eighteenth Amendment would mean the emergence of the cities as the dominant force in America, dominant politically and socially as they are already dominant economically.

The alignment of the new cities against the older villages traverses the nominal political alignment of the two great parties. In New York State, for example, it has divided and broken the Republican Party as a state organization. There is much more community of thought and feeling between Republicans and Democrats in New York City, in Buffalo, Rochester, Syracuse, and Albany, than there is between the urban and the rural Republicans. The unity of the Republican Party in New York is like the unity of the Democrats in the nation: a unity of politicians interested in offices supplemented by the prestige of a name and a tradition. There is no unity of interest, of principle, or of programme.

A similar condition exists in almost every state where there are powerful cities — in Massachusetts for Boston, in Pennsylvania for Pittsburgh and Philadelphia, in Ohio for Cleveland and Cincinnati, in Illinois for Chicago, in New Jersey for that urban conglomeration known as Hudson County, in Missouri for St. Louis. Both parties are cracking under the strain. Both maintain the appearance of unity by political deals and the compromise of principles. The well-known fact that parties have become meaningless is due to this internal division. They dare not take definite positions for fear of alienating one or the other of their irreconcilable factions.

For reasons which are not altogether clear the conflict has first become overt in the Democratic Party. The convention of 1924 was the scene of the first great, though inconclusive, phase of the struggle. All the signs indicate that the next phase, in 1928, will be at least as sharp and perhaps more decisive. In 1924 the urban democracy rallied around Governor Smith of New York, the village democracy around Mr. McAdoo. The urban Democrats in 1924 controlled a little more than one third of that convention. Since 1924 they have gained in strength and by 1928 they should control at least half of the convention. This change of their position from a minority to a majority faction is not due to the personality or to the leadership of Governor Smith. It is due to a growth of self-consciousness which is developing the latent strength of the city electorates. They are beginning to feel their oats. They are throwing off their sense of inferiority. They are beginning to demand the recognition which is due their intrinsic importance.

The outcome of the struggle within the Democratic Party is, of course, obscure. One can be certain of nothing except that the rapid growth of the cities at the expense of the country-side is bound at last to result in the political domination of the cities. This may come soon. It may be somewhat delayed. It will come. The first great result may be the disunion of the Democratic Party and perhaps even the rupture of the Solid South. If that is the result the ascendancy of the Republicans may be temporarily confirmed, but it will be followed almost certainly by a realignment of Republicans as well as of Democrats.

For the two parties live by taking in each other's washing. The unity of the one is dependent upon the unity of the other. The grip of the Eastern industrial Republicans on the national organization rests at last on the fact that in the South there is a Republican machine but no Republican electorate. If ever the South should break away from the Democrats, a Republican Party would appear in the South. The appearance of a Republican Party in the South would make the South as unmanageable to the Republicans of the Northeast as the Republican Party of the West now is.

These prospects are not alluring to men whose lives are bound up with the existing party system. They promise nothing but trouble for them personally. They call for an effort of thought which is distressing, and they open up issues for which political leaders, trained between 1890 and 1910, are not prepared. It is not surprising, then, that our political leaders are greatly occupied in dampening down interest, in obscuring issues, and in attempting to distract attention from the realities of American life.

CHAPTER 5

The Election
of 1928

The first four selections in this chapter, all from *The Nation*,
capture some of the charges and counter-charges in one of
the most acrimonious campaigns in American political history.
The issue for Bishop James Cannon, Jr. of the Methodist Epis-
copal Church, South, was a simple one — the personality of
Governor Al Smith. Cannon, an ardent prohibition leader,
was the subject of Virginius Dabney's critical biography, *Dry
Messiah*. Mary Kingsbury Simkhovitch, author of the re-
joinder to Cannon, was a nationally prominent leader in social
work who served for many years as head worker of Green-
wich House, New York City. An editorial of August 8 calls
attention to a consideration often obscured by the campaign
rhetoric: there were no genuine issues in 1928 since on major
questions of public policy the two parties were virtually in
complete agreement. In the same context, W. E. B. Du Bois,
editor of *The Crisis* and one of the most distinguished of American Negro leaders, notes another neglected aspect of the
1928 campaign. Negro voters throughout the United States,
growing restive in their traditional Republican allegiance, had
been abandoned by the Republicans, and Governor Smith,
fearful of the power of the Solid South, made no bid to win
their support.

It is clear, however, that Smith did not lose because he was a wet or a Catholic. Richard Hofstadter has observed: "A little thoughtful attention to the history of the 1920's will convince almost any student that there was not a Democrat alive, Protestant or Catholic, who could have beaten Hoover in 1928." To argue otherwise is to overlook the economic prosperity of the twenties, the popularity of Herbert Hoover and, most important, the impotence of the Democratic party.

The concluding selection is a statistical analysis of the 1928 results by two University of Chicago sociologists, William F. Ogburn and Nell Snow Talbot. Measuring the significance of five determinants of voting behavior, the authors found the wet–dry variable to be the best indicator of the actual presidential vote. The stronger the opposition to prohibition in any county, they concluded, the greater the vote for Al Smith. Their conclusions, incidentally, differ from those of Samuel Lubell who contends in his well-known book, *The Future of American Politics* (Third edition, revised, New York: Harper & Row, 1965), that the trend toward the Democrats in metropolitan centers, particularly among the foreign born in 1928, was the first step in the shaping of the triumphant Roosevelt coalition, the new Democratic party alignment that was to assure that party's political dominance from 1932 to the present.

JAMES   CANNON,   JR.
Al Smith — Catholic, Tammany, Wet, *The Nation*, 127, July 4, 1928, p. 10

If it were necessary to explain this in a single sentence, I should say: Governor Smith is personally, ecclesiastically, aggressively, irreconcilably Wet, and is ineradicably Tammany-branded, with all the inferences and implications and objectionable consequences which naturally follow from such views and associations. In the issue of *The Nation* of November 30, in an article discussing Governor Smith as a "Presidential possibility," Mr. Villard said:

> Do you believe in electing to the Presidency a man who drinks too much for his own good, and is politically a rampant Wet? . . . Does "Al" drink and does he drink too much? Well, I am reliably informed that he drinks every day, and the number of his cocktails and highballs is variously estimated at from four to eight. It is positively denied that he is ever intoxicated, much gossip to the contrary notwithstanding. He is a Wet, and he lives up to it, and for that consistency he is to be praised. . . . One may regret with all one's heart, as does the writer of these lines, that, being in an exalted position, he cannot set an example of abstinence to the millions whose State he governs, but at least one knows where he stands.

It is now over six months since that statement concerning Governor Smith's personal habits was printed and quoted, and there has been no official denial of its accuracy. It coincides with the private statements of other reliable persons. The facts certainly appear to warrant the asking of this question: Shall Dry America, a country with prohibition imbedded in its Constitution, elect a "cocktail President"?

It is true that a man's personal attitude towards the prohibition amendment and toward the use of intoxicants is not the only important question to be asked concerning his fitness for the office of President of the United States. But one's personal opinion on the principle of prohibition cannot be considered apart from the broader question of loyalty to the Constitution, as long as the prohibition amendment is a part of that Constitution. Furthermore, while it is true that the prohibition amendment does not prohibit the use of intoxicating liquor for beverage purposes, it is also true that it is the natural, logical consequence of the prohibition law that within a comparatively short time all legal use of beverage intoxicants will be eliminated. There are doubtless some law-abiding citizens who still use no intoxicants except those which they possessed at the time that prohibition went into effect, but that number is small and steadily decreasing. Can any law-abiding American citizen want a man to be elected President who not only disbelieves in the principle of prohibition, but, although sworn to uphold the Constitution of the United States, yet will continue to indulge his appetite for strong drink in the Executive Mansion? What an interesting public document for future generations to inspect would be the application of the President of the United States for a permit from the Prohibition Department to move from his residence to the White House an itemized list of the bottles, casks, barrels, and other containers of intoxicating liquor, traffic in which is prohibited by the Constitution which the said applicant is sworn to uphold!

But not only is Governor Smith personally Wet today, but his entire record is Wet. He was a frequenter of saloons while they existed; he put his foot on the brass rail and blew the foam off the glass; in his social and political activities he recognized the saloon as an important factor. As a legislator he not only opposed every measure to restrict the privileges of saloons, but endeavored to remove existing restrictions. He fought the ratification of the Eighteenth Amendment and the passage of the Mullen-Gage State Law Enforcement Code, and after that code had been enacted by the New York State Legislature, he labored aggressively and persistently to obtain its repeal. He is now advocating modifications of the prohibition laws to permit each State to determine what shall be the legal alcoholic content of the beverages permitted.

When all his background is considered, it is not surprising that Governor Smith should have persistently and aggressively fought prohibition. Tammany-bred, a pupil, a follower, a protege of Croker, Foley, and Murphy, he is today the outstanding personality and most influential factor in Tammany Hall. It is true that Mr. George Olvany, the titular head of Tammany Hall, declared on oath before the Senate Committee that Tammany was not a political organization at all, but simply a "patriotic society." But whatever it be called Tammany is, as was declared in *The Nation* for June 13, a "society held together by the cohesive power of public plunder." Governor Smith has for thirty-three years been a worker in or an official of that society. Nor has he condemned the Tammany graft and corruption which has recently come to light. Indeed, he has only recently been reinstated as a sachem.

Moreover, Governor Smith is ecclesiastically Wet. There was published in the secular press on January 2, 1928, a quotation which has not been denied from the *Osservatore Romano*, the official organ of the Vatican, stating that "the attempt to enforce prohibition in America has become so useless, not to say dangerous, that it would be better to abolish it, especially since unbridled passion is always more rampant as soon as there is an attempt to enforce complete abstinence." This attack upon the prohibition law of the United States by the Vatican organ is in full agreement with the open criticism of that law by the Cardinal Archbishop of New York and Boston and other Roman Catholic dignitaries.

I concede the right of the Pope, cardinals, archbishops, and other Roman Catholics to declare their attitude as freely as Methodist, Baptist, Presbyterian, or other Protestant bodies or ministers or laymen upon this question. Nor would I even intimate that these Roman Catholic leaders are not sincere in their opposition to the prohibition law. But it is not surprising, indeed it is to be expected, that this position of high dignitaries of the Roman church will be reflected in the attitude of many loyal Catholics who are members of legislatures, or of Congress, or who hold other official positions. It is a fact that the attacks in Congress upon the prohibition law are made chiefly by men who are themselves Roman Catholics or who represent constituencies with large Roman Catholic populations. Certainly it is likely that Governor Alfred E. Smith is influenced by the views of the Pope and the cardinals on the subject of prohibition.

I repeat that because Governor Smith is personally, ecclesiastically, aggressively, irreconcilably Wet and is ineradicably

Tammany-branded, the South's Dry Democrats will oppose him. It is unthinkable that the moral, religious leadership of the South could be a party to the nomination or election of such a man as Governor Smith, thus being guilty of an open betrayal of a great social, economic, and moral reform which was won after years of unselfish labor. If the Houston convention should nominate Governor Smith for President, multiplied thousands of life-long Democrats will decide that Democracy will be better served by the defeat of the Wet Tammany sachem than by his election, and will act accordingly.

MARY KINGSBURY SIMKHOVITCH
Al Smith — Able, Honest, Liberal, *The Nation*, 127, *July 4, 1928, pp. 9–10*

Being neither a Roman Catholic nor a member of Tammany Hall nor of Irish descent, I am for Smith for President. I do not think that a Catholic is less loyal than a Protestant. Experience is the safest guide. Catholic Supreme Court justices, Senators, and governors have not done us any harm. In fact. the conscious or unconscious desire to class our country as Protestant seems to be at variance with our fundamental law which provides for entire freedom of belief.

The three main objections to Smith are: first, that he is Wet; second, that he is a member of Tammany Hall; and third, that business is safer with a Republican than with a Democratic administration no matter who the candidates are.

The cause of temperance was making great headway when we adopted prohibition. We have now had almost a decade of experience to go on, and no one will deny that the natural result of any prohibition has taken place. The educational process has been replaced by lawlessness. We did not know as much ten years ago about psychology as we do today. Progressive educational ideas, replacing the "thou shalt nots" with positive outlets in the emotional and intellectual life,

are now understood more widely. Just as recreational and vocational opportunities are stressed to offset juvenile delinquency
rather than a reliance on reformatories and jails, so is education
in self-control superior to prohibition. If prohibition is bad
social psychology, we must face this fact and ask how it can
be honestly met. Governor Smith has not concealed his views
on this subject. Is it not possible to take a dispassionate attitude on a question of public policy? Is it necessary to brand
any one who desires a modification of the law as unpatriotic
or dangerous? Fanaticism, wholly out of keeping with our
fundamental constitutional rights, lies in that direction. To
enforce the law completely will not be possible for any President, unless Congress votes a sum of money no practical person believes can be obtained. That Smith, if President, would
not enforce the law as strictly as funds available would allow,
no one believes who knows him and his work intimately.

Smith is a loyal member of Tammany Hall. All organizations have their weak spots. But to make a wholesale indictment of Tammany Hall is to indict the Democratic Party in
the city of New York, which is the same as to indict the majority of its citizens. Tammany Hall has had an honorable
record as well as a discreditable one. People are members of
the organization by neighborly association — I was about to
say, almost by the accident of birth. In a sense it is like a
large family or clan life, full of mistakes and worse, but also
full of sympathy, effective helpfulness, and an intensely real-
istic understanding of what is practical. Before the social psy-
chologists got busy in their interpretations, Tammany Hall
practiced what later the sociologists taught.

Now, Smith was brought up with this crowd. And he is
loyal to it as he is loyal to his family, to his church, to his
neighborhood, to his city, and to his State. Dependability
and clear-sightedness are his major qualities. And he never
confuses loyalty, as so many bigots do, with blind agreement
and objection to criticism. A real loyalty includes criticism.
And that he has given Tammany Hall plenty of it is an open

secret. But he has given it from the inside rather than from the outside. That is a legitimate way. "Boring from within" is as reputable a method as opposition from without. Smith has never side-stepped a burden or discarded a responsibility. He has never taken the easier way.

It is often easier to leave a church or family life or a political party than it is to stick and see what changes in these social structures can be effected. All organization is full of defects. The price we pay for it is heavy but in general necessary. I do not say that to get out, to bolt, is not a good way sometimes, too. But that is a question of when and why and how. Smith chooses the old-fashioned, responsible way of sticking.

Finally, there is the argument of prosperity. Many will vote for a Democratic governor who won't vote for a Democratic President. Their idea is that change is disorganizing and disintegrating for business and hence for the country. But though economic security is a primary issue and on it depends a high level in the standard of living, there is to be considered as an even more fundamental issue the whole tone of American life — its regard for honesty in public service, its old emphasis on local responsibility and initiative, its regard for the welfare of the downmost groups which business prosperity has not touched, its ancient privilege of criticism in public life, which the long-continued term in office of any party tends to obscure.

When the Progressive Party of Roosevelt's day went out of business it left the Democratic Party as its only residuary legatee in the field of practical and effective social-minded public criticism. Smith is obviously its ablest leader. With his usual sagacity and common sense, he will by no means desire to kill the goose that lays the golden egg. If he is elected we may therefore expect a maximum of fresh air in political thought and action, with no worry that prosperity will fly out of the window.

As Like as Two Peas, *The Nation, 127, August 8, 1928, p. 122*

That is what the two older political parties have become —
as like as two peas. They have been tending in this direction
for years, as *The Nation* has long been pointing out. But in
this campaign we are getting frank admissions of this fact
from quarters in which the effort has hitherto been made to
convince the voters that there really were radical differences
between what the Republicans and Democrats stood for. Walter Lippmann of the New York *World* was quite open about
it in his radio debate the other night with Ogden L. Mills,
the Assistant Secretary of the Treasury. The only difference
between the two platforms on foreign affairs, Mr. Lippmann
admitted, was that while both were voluble and vague the
Republican took longer to read. Both mean about the same
thing, for, he said, "both were written by men determined to
use the largest words with the smallest meaning." As for
William Allen White, he is quite cynical, not to say ribald,
about it. The Republicans, he declares, sighed over corruption
and "the Democrats yelled about it at the top of their voices."
As for prohibition, the Republicans were for its enforcement
"in a gentlemanly way"; the Democrats "evaded as far as
they dared the promise to enforce the Volstead Act." For
the rest, according to the doctrine in Emporia:

> On farm relief the Republicans heaved a sigh at the sad state
> of the farmer, and promised him exactly what the Democrats
> have promised, except that with their promise the Democrats
> gave the farmer three lusty cheers. On other matters — except-
> ing the tariff, wherein each party was traditional, neither being
> really excited about it — both parties were explicit without en-
> thusiasm. But speaking broadly, one may say that if the Repub-
> lican platform is the sublimation of a silent tear, the Democratic
> platform is a passionate straddle in white pants.

If Mr. Lippmann and Mr. White are not quite fair in some
respects — the Democrats abandoned at Houston their historic tariff position, while the Democratic planks on foreign

policy are distinctly more liberal and anti-imperialistic than
the Repubican — a prominent official of the Wilson Administration has admitted privately that, with the surrender of the
Democrats on the tariff and their indifference to the League
of Nations, there is now no worth-while distinction between
the two parties. "It has come down," he declares, "to the
simple decision whether you prefer the man Hoover to the
man Smith." This is more to the point because of the determined effort to make it appear that Smith is no more dangerous
to business than is Hoover. Mr. Olvany, the head of Tammany
Hall, did not wait to return to New York before issuing a
statement from the train that business had nothing whatever
to fear from Smith. More than that, for the first time in years
a Democratic banner has been hung in Wall Street. It cer-
tifies to the support of Alfred E. Smith by the business men's
association of the lower part of that historic thoroughfare.
But the thing does not stop there. Governor Smith has himself chosen the chairman of the board of General Motors as
his campaign manager, while William H. Woodin, president
of the American Car and Foundry Company, has also joined
the Democratic forces.

What matters it beside this that a college president from
the South, a former Senator from Oklahoma, and a Democratic committee-woman from Maine have joined the Hoover
forces? What the Democrats are doing is muzzling the Republican orators who usually assure the country that the Democrats are certain to upset all business if their candidate is
elected. Obviously they cannot do that when Judge Olvany,
Colonel Herbert H. Lehman, Mr. Raskob, Mr. Woodin, and
the Lower Wall Street Business Men's Association are there
to certify that Governor Smith's election will not injure what
is left of Coolidge prosperity. This is certainly a new role
for the Democratic Party. It is thus no longer the defender
of the small business man, the protagonist of the worker, the
sworn protector of the plain people who suffer from the
money power and the trusts. It has forgotten that only six-
teen years ago that Democratic President who was so highly

praised at the Houston convention chose for the keynote of
his successful campaign for the White House the fact that
"the masters of the government of the United States are the
combined capitalists and manufacturers of the United States."
In addition he insisted that "the government of the United
Stats at present is a foster-child of the special interests. It is
not allowed to have a will of its own," and he declared that
through him and the Democratic Party the government would
be taken away from "the big manufacturers, the bankers, and
the heads of the great railroad combinations."

The truth is that this apostasy of the Democratic Party
is a sorry business for the voters. There still are vital issues
before the American people. What is happening is that both
candidates for the Presidency are kowtowing to the business
powers that control. When Governor Smith's backers portray him as safe and sane for all business they picture him as
faithless to the soundest tenets of the Democracy. He ought
not to be safe and sane for all business. He ought to be as
dreaded by lawless business and that portion of the business
world which is seeking to acquire certain birthrights of the
American people as was Woodrow Wilson when he was putting through his "Seven Sisters" laws against the corporations
in New Jersey. For the Democracy of Grover Cleveland to
support the tariff and to pretend that the organization is like
the Republican Party in all its aims and ambitions is indeed
to reduce the whole business to a question of personality, to
whether you like Al Smith's brown derby or prefer Mr.
Hoover's conventional straw hat; whether you prefer to have
Mrs. Hoover in the White House rather than Mrs. Smith;
whether you think that Smith's election would or would not
turn over the United States government to the Pope. All the
vast problems of capitalism and labor are shoved aside; no issues are defined on vital foreign problems.

It is still true, of course, that the candidates may make sharp
issues if they will. But on what? Prohibition? Mr. Hoover
has spent nearly seven and one-half years in two Administra-

tions neither of which has made the slightest real effort to enforce prohibition. Neither will Mr. Hoover do so if he is elected. In the end the question still is: Do you like Smith better than Hoover? There is no difference whatever between their parties.

W . E . BURGHARDT DU BOIS
Is Al Smith Afraid of the South? *The Nation*, *127*, *October 17*, *1928*, *pp. 392–394*

Alfred Smith is not the first American politician for whom the Negroes of the United States have proved a most embarrassing stumbling block. But seldom have the implications of this situation been so clear to all Americans who are willing to think.

Mr. Smith is posing as liberal. His attitude toward superpower, toward non-partisan appointments to office, and toward prohibition give him some color of right to this definition. Toward the greater and ever more pressing problems of the distribution of income and ownership of property, he is making tentative approach by noting the economic distress of the American farmer. But all this does not prove his case, and does not make his appeal to American liberals by any means clear; for he has also made desperate effort to reassure intrenched American capital that he cannot be counted as its enemy; that he will be considerate of corporations like General Motors; and that he will take care of the interests intrenched behind the tariff. All this would make liberal support of Mr. Smith debatable. But there is another matter where there can be no debate.

Mr. Smith is silent about the Negro. Why? Certainly it is not because he has no need of the Negro vote. Migration from South to North, and from country to city, has increased the effective vote which Negroes cast very appreciably over 1916, and considerably over 1920 and 1924. We must, of course, depend upon estimates instead of actual figures, but in States where the real battles of this campaign are apparently being fought, there is a large Negro vote: in New York, 150,000; in New Jersey, 75,000; in Ohio, 125,000; in Indiana, 75,000; in Illinois, 175,000; in West Virginia, 50,000; in Kentucky, 125,000; in Tennessee, 225,000; in North Carolina, 25,-000; in California, 40,000. Even Massachusetts has 21,000 voters, and Connecticut, 15,000. There are probably 60,000 Negro voters in Michigan and 125,000 in Missouri. Kansas has 35,000, Delaware, 15,000, and Maryland, 140,000. Of course, in the Southern hinterland, there is little chance that any appreciable Negro vote will be cast or counted. And yet in Virginia, South Carolina, Georgia, Florida, Texas, and Oklahoma the Negro vote of 100,000 might conceivably be of importance if any real rift were made in the governing oligarchy.

This is an asset that no astute politician — and no one has accused Mr. Smith of not being astute — would ordinarily neglect. Moreover, the Negroes are incensed against the Republican Party and against Mr. Hoover as never before. Some defection from the ranks of Negro Republicans was felt as early as 1912, and Woodrow Wilson went out of his way to encourage it. He openly promised Negroes "Justice and not mere grudging justice." Led by the late Bishop Alexander Walters, a Negro bureau was established at Democratic headquarters and a considerable Negro vote was cast for Woodrow Wilson. But the Wilson administration disappointed Negroes even more than it disappointed other people. Wilson refused to appoint the fact finding commission which he had promised to Oswald Garrison Villard; he refused to recognize the Negro in any important appointments; his whole Negro program succumbed to the Southern oligarchy, except during the war scare. By 1916 the revolt was well over and Negroes went back and voted with docility for Mr. Hughes.

In 1920, Cox made no appeal to the colored vote and it went almost solidly for Harding. In 1924, however, revolt

began again. Davis was a favorite among West Virginia Negroes, and led by William H. Lewis, the Boston lawyer, many
colored voters bolted Coolidge. But all this revolt was as
nothing to that which was brewing among Negroes in 1928.
If Al Smith would raise a finger to assure American Negroes
that, while he was not necessarily a warm friend, at least he
could not be classed as an enemy, he would receive more Negro votes than any Democrat has ever received. For the first
time in the history of colored Republican politics, leading
colored politicians, like R. R. Church of Tennessee, refused
to serve upon the colored Advisory Committee; the head of
the Negro Elks openly pledged his organization against Hoover,
and there was every sign that the defection thus begun was
going to reach large proportions.

Nor were the reasons for this far to see. If leading Negroes
repudiated Coolidge in 1924, they were even more estranged
in 1928. Moreover, Hoover's silence on them and their problems has been nearly as great as Smith's. He has said not a
single public word against lynching or disfranchisement or
for Negro education and uplift. When it was brought to his
attention that the Red Cross was discriminating outrageously
against Negroes suffering from the Mississippi flood, Hoover
at first denied it vehemently; afterward he named a Negro
committee of his friends, headed by R. R. Moton of Tuskegee,
and when this committee confirmed the evidences of discrimination he refused to let the committee publish its findings.

In addition to this, Hoover has joined openly with the "Lily
Whites" of the South, — that is, with those active Southern
politicians who propose, not simply to keep the Southern
Negro disfranchised, but to prevent the organization of any
effecive minority party in which the Negro has representation.
Hoover knows perfectly well that the disfranchisement of
the better class Negroes in the South delivers them into the
hands of venal politicians, black and white. Hoover, Coolidge,
Hughes, Harding, and all Republican candidates receive gladly
the political support of these men in the national conventions.

After the convention, Mr. Hoover proceeds to recognize only the white politicians who have supported him. It was very easy to find evidence for accusing Southern Negro politicians of traffic in public office. But the same accusations have been made and proven against white politicians. There is no reason to think that the accusations were any more true in the case of the colored Perry Howard than in the case of the white Bascom Slemp, once Secretary to President Coolidge. But under Hoover's political organization Howard was kicked out and prosecuted, while Slemp was put in charge of his Southern campaign! Every Negro political leader in the South regardless of his standing — and there are some who are honest and brave — has been unceremoniously ousted by Hoover and his lieutenants.

Here, then, was a chance and an unusual chance for Al Smith, and not simply a chance for political maneuvering. It was a chance to attack in its stronghold the central danger of American democracy; the thing that makes it impossible for the American people today to vote logically or coherently on any subject whatsoever; and that incubus is the bloc of 114 to 139 electoral votes which are out of politics in the sense that no political discussion, no appeal to intelligence or justice, has any influence on them. This was the time for a really great statement. The Governor of New York might have stepped into the arena and said: "I believe in democracy. I believe that poverty and misfortune, even if coupled with slavery and color, are in themselves no reason for caste and disfranchisement. If in spite of misfortune, poverty, and handicap a man meets the qualifications laid down for voting, he ought to vote and to be protected in his vote. He and his ought not to be interfered with by lawlessness and lynching. Education and encouragement ought freely to be offered, and every opportunity for development placed before such people."

Is there any reason why any American citizen, Democrat, Republican, or Socialist, should not subscribe to such a creed and publicly announce it? If there is, then American democracy is already a failure. If there is not, then Alfred Smith ought to have made such a statement. Moreover, I violate no confidence in saying that he was asked and urged to do it and that he refused.

A number of enthusiastic colored folk and friends of colored people put before the advisors of Governor Smith several possible statements which he might make to show that at least he was not an enemy of the American Negro. He refused to say a single word. He refused to let even indirectly anything go out from his headquarters which should seem to represent him as friendly to black men. Negro Democratic headquarters were indeed established but they were not allowed to have offices in the regular Democratic headquarters but were given a small "Jim Crow" annex where they exist without real authority, without explicit recognition, and without the slightest initiative.

On the other hand, explicit and repeated anti-Negro propaganda is being sent out by Democratic headquarters. When the Klan accused Governor Smith of having as his private stenographer "a Negro wench," Democratic headquarters at Washington on September 8 sent out the following release:

> Governor Smith does not have, and never has had, a Negro stenographer, and in the employment of Negroes by the State of New York under his administration this has been done only to fill such jobs as they are given in the South, to wit: porters, janitors, charwomen, etc.

The interesting thing about this statement is that it is perfectly true. In all Governor Smith's long career, he has sedulously avoided recognizing Negroes in any way. He has twice vetoed bills which would have given a colored magistrate to Harlem. He has never given a Negro any major appointment. He has seldom been willing to receive a Negro delegation and it is doubtful if he has met personally in all his career a half-dozen of the 250,000 Negroes of his State.

At one time the leaders of his party in New York City recommended that the late Colonel Charles Young be made head of the new Negro regiment authorized under the direction of the Democratic Governor Sulzer. This regiment had not been organized because of the question of colored officers. The State National Guard was determined that there should be no colored officers, and gave as an excuse that none was qualified. But Charles Young, then a Major in the regular army and a West Point graduate, was a man not only of stainless personal character, but of well-known ability. The army would have been perfectly willing to lend him to the National Guard. Governor Smith was asked to appoint him. He peremptorily refused and placed a white man at the head of the colored 15th Regiment.

Now why should a man otherwise in many respects liberal and likable, who has himself come up from the common people, show himself so illiberal and petty toward the Negro? It is because Smith has been afraid of the South, and is so today. He probably first ignored the Negro because, with East Side ignorance, he knew nothing about him, and shared the East Side's economic dislike of Negro labor competition: a dislike which was back of the Irish anti-Negro riots before and during the war, in Philadelphia and New York. As Smith began to develop in political power and ambition, he recognized that if he wanted to carry the South he must be orthodox on the Negro according to Southern traditions. He has been so, and, in the future, according to Congressman Hill of Alabama, "Governor Smith says he will let us handle the Negro problem as we see fit. What more could we ask?" Then, again, his liquor program and his religion have stirred up enough trouble and revolt south of the Mason and Dixon line. Smith is determined, therefore, not to say a single word that will enable his enemies and the Ku Klux Klan to fasten the title "Nigger-lover" upon him.

This is unfortunate for the Negro. But it is far more unfortunate for the American people. It means that no attempt to liberalize either the Republican or the Democratic Party, or to start a new third-party movement, can succeed as long as the present disfranchisement of the Negro supports a Solid South. Few Americans yet realize this. Many simple souls have a distinct hope that the Democratic Party may yet figure as a liberal party. They have an additional hope that it will never be necessary in the future, as it has not seemed necessary to these liberals in the past, to take any stand or attitude with regard to the so-called Negro problem. They propose to go on, ignoring the fact that the eleven Southern States, with an increase of population of more than 200 per cent since 1870, and with a theoretical doubling of the electorate by woman suffrage, did not, between the election of 1872 and that of 1924, increase its voting population more than 131 per cent, and that in five States of the Southern South the voting population has actually decreased in fifty years. In other words, a rotten borough system has been built up in the South which has disfranchised 5,000,000 voters and put the political power of a third of the nation in the hands of fewer than a million voters!

The political power of this rump electorate is astonishing. They send forty-five congressmen to Washington, while a million voters on the Pacific Coast send but twelve! They keep their Congressmen in office for long periods, thus enabling the South to monopolize a large number of the chief committee appointments. What chance is there that this political power will become radical or even liberal? Not the slightest. Now and then we may get some wild talk from Tillman or Jeff Davis or Caraway. You may get gestures from Carter Glass and taunts from Pat Harrison and solemn rhodomontades from Swanson of Virginia. But when it comes to votes, in every case the Solid South will be found to be the tail of the conservative reactionary North, and not a single reform movement, no punishment of swindlers, no real investigation of political evils, can depend upon Southern support. The Solid South cannot be liberal. It is built upon the disfranchisement, not only of 2,000,000 Negroes, but of many more than 2,000,000 whites. It is built on widespread ignorance and intolerance; crime and lynching; peonage and slavery. Its business is to choke off all discussion among liberal whites

in the South; to stop all political independence, social freedom, or religious liberalism. For any sane liberal in the United
States to think that this body of death is going to be per-
meated by liberal opinions is clear evidence of incipient soft-
ening of the brain.

If now the Southern Democratic bloc cannot become liberal,
what chance is there that the Northern Democrats will become liberal? None at all. In Northern States they may temporarily follow liberal principles. But nationally they must
do as Smith has done: make peace with plutocracy and repu-
diate the simplest principles of democracy.

There are a number of hopeful souls who continue to believe that the very ineptitude of the two old parties is going
to lead, one of these days, to a triumphant third party. These
dreamers insist that this already would have happened if third
party advocates could only "agree." This is nonsense. When
and where have liberal reformers ever agreed in advance on
main matters of reform? Certainly not at the birth of the Republican Party in the United States or at the birth of the
Liberal or Labor Party in England. Widely divergent liberal
panaceas are slowly pounded into shape at successive elections
as certain of them gain popular support. By a slow process
of selection and elimination, the program of a third party
is clarified and solidified, and slowly one of the old parties
dies. This program is impossible in the United States because
the one political party, the Democrats, which is nearest mori-
bund in its ideas, cannot die; it uses the political power of
disfranchised Negroes and disfranchised whites to keep itself
so large a minority party that any diversion of liberals from
the Republican Party simply throws this more reactionary
party into power. That was the clear case in the celebrated
election of 1912. It was the largest influence in the election of
Coolidge, when at the last moment voters became convinced
that a vote for La Follette was practically a vote for the
Democrats.

The same situation is before us today. Liberals may, if they
will, vote for Al Smith. But a vote for Al Smith is a vote

for the Bourbon South, and that reactionary bloc will not let Smith take a single really liberal step. They will stand with the Republicans for super-power, for high protection, for disfranchisement, and for war made by an army and navy which they overwhelmingly dominate. On the other hand, if the liberals turn and vote for Norman Thomas they throw their votes away just as surely as when they voted for Robert La Follette. Under the present distribution of electoral votes Norman Thomas has no chance of carrying a single State even if he should receive 6,000,000 popular votes. All of which shows that the problem of Negro disfranchisement is not a problem of the Negroes; it is a problem of democratic government in the United States.

WILLIAM   F.   OGBURN
AND   NELL   SNOW   TALBOT

A Measurement of the Factors in the Presidential Election of 1928, *Social Forces, VIII, December 1929, pp. 175–183*

[*A correlation coefficient, as the term is employed in this article, is a measure of relationship between two variables, that is, the percent vote for Smith and the percent in the same county opposed to prohibition. If the two variables were perfectly synchronized and increased and decreased precisely the same, the resulting correlation coefficient would be 1.00. If the two variables were in no way related, the resulting coefficient would be .0. Since five variables are involved in the analysis of the Smith vote (designated as X_1), the technique involved is referred to as "multivariate analysis." The authors have compiled "partial correlations" among all of the five variables as well as a coefficient of multiple correlation, the combined effect of all five variables on X_1. Since the true results of the election were known by the authors, they were able to reach their conclusions as to the respective weight of the variables by noting which single variable or combination of variables best predicted the actual results.*

Unfortunately subsequent research in statistics casts doubt upon conclusions reached in this 1929 article. The authors run afoul the "ecological fallacy" when they infer the behavior of individual voters from the total vote for a particular county. It is statistically plausible, for example, that in a county where 60% of the voters opposed prohibition and 60% voted for Smith that the 40% who favored prohibition might have actually voted for Smith.]

I

It is generally thought that in the presidential election of 1928 the Democratic candidate was strongly supported by the foreign-born vote, by the wets, by the Catholics, by the cities, and by the regular Democrats. It is likewise believed that the Republican candidate was supported by the opposites of these forces. There is apparently some truth in these claims, but one might be interested in knowing more. For instance it would be interesting to know whether the Catholic influence was stronger than that of the wets on the Democratic vote, or whether the foreign-born supported Smith more strongly than the urbanist; but it would not be easy to give an answer. For often the Smith supporters dwelt in cities and the same persons were at the same time foreign born, wet, Catholic, and regular Democrats. The eggs are scrambled, so to speak. And it is difficult to separate the yolks from the whites, once they have been scrambled. (If it were necessary, no doubt some inventor would make a separator such as has been made for milk and cream.) In the case of politics, it is desired to present here such a separator of issues and to show what are the results when it is applied to the recent election for president of the United States.

How these issues may be separated will now be shown. If a certain number of counties could be found in which there were exactly the same percentages of foreign born, of wets, of regular Democrats, of city people, but with differing percentages of Catholics, then we could take some of these counties that had, say, 20 per cent of Catholics and compare the votes for Smith with those in certain other counties that had, say, 30 per cent of Catholics. Perhaps the Smith vote in the latter counties might average 3 per cent greater than in the former. We would then say that an increase in 10 per cent of the Catholics in a county increased the Smith vote by 3 per cent, when the other aforementioned factors were the same in the counties.

Similarly it might be found in counties that had exactly the same percentages of foreign-born, of Catholics, of regular Democrats, and of city people but with differing percentages of wets, that an increase of 10 per cent in the wets increased the Smith vote by 4 per cent.

If such results were found we should be justified in saying that the wet influence, unmixed with these other influences, on the Smith vote was greater than the Catholic influence alone. In the same way other forces operating in the campaign could be isolated and measured. It is not practicable to locate these counties in actuality where all these factors are exactly the same except the one to be varied. But it is possible to select for study a group of random counties with varying percentages of all these influences and by the procedures of partial differentiation and of the method of least squares to hold all of the factors constant but the one which is varied and thus come to the same achievement that would be reached if counties could be located having exactly the same percentages of the various influences except the one to be studied.

This has been done for 173 counties located at random in the following states[1] of the North and West, Massachusetts, New York, Ohio, Illinois, Wisconsin, Colorado, Montana, and

---

[1] These particular states were chosen because they were the only ones which had voted on some form of the wet-dry issue and hence for which an index of wetness could be obtained. The counties were chosen at random except that certain counties were eliminated in order to make the frequency distributions of the various indexes of factors approximately symmetrical, a result desired for the technical purpose of getting the relationships expressed in linear form. The numbers of cities in the

California. The results of the analysis are shown below. The figures indicate the percentages of change in the Democratic vote when there is a ten per cent increase in the particular factor named, the percentages of all the other factors listed above being the same. These figures then represent the ranking from the least to the greatest of the five factors (as defined) in the recent presidential election, each one being independent of the others.

Factors which are increased 10 per cent in the counties	The corresponding percentage increases in the Democratic vote
Foreign born	0.5
Urban population[2]	0.8 (decrease)
Democratic voters[3]	1.8
Catholics	2.8
Wet voters[4]	4.1

The wet influence is seen to be greater than the Catholic influence, that is, a 10 per cent increase in the number of wet voters increases the Smith vote more than does a 10 per cent increase in the Catholics.[5] Some interpreters of the election

counties of varying populations of over 10,000 inhabitants are shown in the following table:

Sizes of Cities	Number of Cities
10,000– 50,000	148
50,000– 100,000	22
100,000– 500,000	15
500,000–1,000,000	4
1,000,000 and over	1
	190

[2] Percentage of the urban population means the percentage of the population living in places of over 2500 inhabitants.

[3] The Democratic voters are measured by the Cox vote in 1920.

[4] The wet voters are those that voted wet in state elections on some form of the wet-dry issue.

[5] The increase in the wets is an increase in the wet voters whereas the increase in the Catholics is an increase in Catholic membership. But it is assumed that the percentage of Catholics is very highly correlated with the percentage of Catholics who are voters.

have seen the religious issue as affecting voters more strongly than the prohibition issue, but this is not the case for these Northern and Western states.

It should be noted that the ranking above measures the force of these factors per unit of size, i.e., per percentage change, rather than the sizes of these factors numerically. For instance, there are many more wets than Catholics. In these counties the average percentage of Catholics was 20 while the average percentage of wet voters was 56.[6] The ratio of the numbers, i.e., percentages, is nearly 1 to 3, (but of course they are not mutually exclusive categories) while the ratio of their influences per unit of size is 1 to 1½.

The influence of the Democratic vote as measured by the Cox vote of 1920 (per percentage of change) was surprisingly small. This is surprising to those of us who are accustomed to thinking of party loyalty as a great conservative force resisting change, as illustrated by the persistence of the solid (nearly) South and of the two parties despite numerous attempts to break them up. The concept of party influence that it was desired to measure is that of voters who vote rather regularly for the party. Such a measure of party regularity would give a smaller result than the normal or average party vote. It would probably have made little difference whether we had taken the Cox vote or the Davis vote as our index since the correlations of these votes with the Smith vote in these counties were the same, +.12 and +.13 respectively. It is indeed very striking how little was the common support in these counties of Smith and Davis and of Smith and Cox.

The influence of the foreign-born vote for Smith is seen to be almost negligible when the influences of religion, prohibition, party, and residence are removed. The foreign-born voted more for Smith than for Hoover for the correlation between the Smith vote and the percentage of foreign-born

---

[6] The comparative size of these factors is shown by the arithmetic means in percentages which are as follows: Smith vote, 38.2; foreign-born, 23:1; Catholics, 19.6; wets, 56.2; Cox vote, 29.8; urban, 54.5.

is $+.33$, but when these other influences are removed the correlation is $+.07$, almost negligible. In other words, the foreign-born voted for Smith because they were wet and Catholic or for some other reason closely correlated with these, and not apparently for the sole reason that they were foreign-born. If there was a clash between the Old American Stock and the newer immigration in the past election, as many magazine writers seemed to think, expecting Smith to lead new hosts as Jackson had done, it would seem from the foregoing coefficient to have been due not so much to nativity as to drink and religion. The foregoing analysis is true for the counties studied, and is probably representative of the United States in general except for the South. But it may be that if large cities alone had been studied, the influence of the foreign-born might have been found to have been greater. We made for instance a correlation between the Smith vote and the percentage of foreign-born in 59 cities of the North and West and the coefficient was $+.56$. The correlation on the basis of counties it is recalled was $+.33$. A somewhat higher correlation was to have been expected since the county is a larger unit than the city. How much this correlation of $+.56$ would have been reduced if the various other factors had been held constant is not known. A study of the vote based on large cities is probably not as representative a method as a study based on counties.

The urban influence was not as strong for Smith as many persons seem to think. Hoover carried many cities and large ones, including Chicago, for instance. Indeed our analysis shows that when the influences of religion, drink, and immigration are removed from the urban influence, it went slightly more for Hoover than for Smith. Even when these influences are not removed, the urban factor was only slightly pro Smith, $(r = +.16)$. The election does not seem to have called forth any special rural or urban influence as such for either side. The dividing line for urban was at places with 2500 inhabitants and over. While this gives a better definition of rural than urban, it is not necessarily a bad relative index of

THE ELECTION OF 1928   203

the urban for our counties. This point is discussed elsewhere
in the paper.

The foregoing ranking of influences which we have just
been discussing is correct for the positions on the scale but
the ratios of one influence to another are not so precise as
they might be because of the unequal variabilities of the percentages.[7] The coefficients of correlation remove this disturb-
ing influence of unequal variabilities and the squares of the
partial coefficients give the best basis for ratios of one influence to another. These squared coefficients (with the digits
of the ten thousandth places omitted and the decimal points
removed) are shown below. The numbers represent then comparative influences of the different factors on the Smith vote,
independent of the others.

Foreign-born influences	5
Rural influences	32
Democratic influences	63
Catholic influences	109
Wet influences	314

The wet influence is the most powerful, nearly three times
as great as the Catholic, which ranks second. The Catholic
influence is about twice as great as the traditional Democratic
party influence, which in turn is twice as great as the rural.
The foreign-born influence is quite neglible.

An interesting question is how many of the influences of
the campaign have we included when we have studied these
five influences of party, religion, prohibition, urban-rural and
immigration. Because unless these comprise a fairly large
percentage, we shall not have gained so much in holding four
of these constant, for there may be other important ones that
we have not held constant. A different ranking might have

---

[7] The standard deviations in percentages are as follows: Smith vote, 8.85;
foreign-born, 10.77; Catholic, 9.22; wet, 11.78; Democratic, 9.80; urban,
21.50.

occurred if we had held other important ones constant. There were other factors, an important one being no doubt the amounts of money spent in the different counties. Another is the extent of activity of the party organization. Other issues were the tariff and the control of consolidated electric power. The five influences here considered, we estimate, comprise 59 per cent ($R_{1.23456} = 0.77$) of the effective influences bearing on the election. We have included, therefore, a fairly large percentage, and when a large percentage of the factors have been held constant, there is less likelihood of a different ranking when additional ones are included.

The reader may be interested in the ranking of the influences when no influences have been held constant. For illustration, the correlation of the wet vote with the Smith vote is $+.65$ when no factors are held constant but is $+.56$ when the four other factors are held constant. In other words, the wets voted for Smith in part because they were Catholic and foreign-born. And when these other influences are removed the correlation of the wet vote with the Smith vote is less. Similar comparisons are shown for the correlations of the other factors with the Smith vote, in correlation coefficients listed below, the second column being those where no factors were held constant and the first column being the partial coefficients.

$+.07$	$+.33$	Foreign-born
$-.18$	$+.16$	Urban
$+.25$	$+.11$	Democrats
$+.33$	$+.47$	Catholics
$+.56$	$+.65$	Wets

It is seen from the above that when the various factors are held constant most of the simple correlations are reduced. This was to have been expected, since the same communities are often wet, Catholic, and foreign-born, and sometimes urban and Democratic. An exception is the case of the correlation of the Smith vote with the traditionally Democratic vote, as measured by the Cox vote of 1920. When the various factors are held constant, the correlation is raised. The forces of the Catholics and of the wets reduced in these counties the normal Democratic group.

The results just described are in part validated by the fact that the basic equation yielding the above mentioned results can be used very successfully to predict the Smith vote. For instance, if the percentages for a county on wetness, on Catholicism, on urbanism, on the Cox vote, and on the foreign-born are furnished us, we can tell the Smith vote in that county within 4 per cent about half the time and two-thirds of the time within less than 6 per cent. (The standard error of estimate is 5.9 per cent.) This statement is quite true for the counties which were the basis of this study. Theoretically not quite such good accuracy of prediction is to be expected on the average for other counties; for it is remembered that the frequency distributions here used were selected so that they were approximately symmetrical, whereas, for the county as a whole they would not all be so. We have tested this point empirically by taking certain counties not used in the study and seeing how well we could predict the Smith vote.

For instance, take DeKalb county, Illinois, a county on which our results were not based. In this county the percentage of foreign-born was 23, the percentage of the population that were Catholics was 7, the percentage wet was 50, the percentage voting for Cox was 14, and the percentage urban was 36. If these values are substituted successively for the Xs in the equation, $X_1 = 6.29 + .052X_2 + .277X_3 + .412X_4 + .181X_5 - .059X_6$ and the equation is solved for X_1, the percentage of votes cast for Smith is calculated to be 30, whereas as a matter of fact the percentage of votes actually cast for Smith was 26. Similarly we have tried the prediction for 31 other counties, not included in our sample of 173 counties, but coming from the same states, none being from the South. In predicting the Smith vote in these 32 counties 50 per cent of the predictions came within 3 per cent of the actual Smith vote. And in nearly seven-eighths of the counties the prediction of the Smith

vote by the equation was within 8 per cent of the percentages
of the actual votes cast for Smith. For five counties the miss
was large, the largest miss being 21 per cent. But in these few
counties where the miss was large some one or two factors
were found to an extremely high or low degree. In general
prediction is not so good for extreme cases, according to the
theory of errors.

The equation based on all five of these factors yields the
best prediction of the election returns in a particular county.
But it is interesting to note that the equation based on the liquor
vote alone $X_1 = 10.98 + .485X_4$ gives very nearly as good
prediction results as does the equation based on the five factors. In fact the best guess as to the Smith strength in a community is the wetness of the community, if only one factor
is considered. The next best guess as to the Smith vote is the
extent of Catholicism. The percentage of foreign-born also
yields a fairly good estimate, but not quite so good as liquor
and Catholicism. The Cox vote was not much of a basis for
predicting, nor was the percentage of persons living in urban
communities.

The preceding analysis represents an unscrambling of some
of the more important of the various influences entering into
the election, and a measurement of the strength of each per
unit of size.

II

In Part I the more interesting results were set forth briefly.
Some of the terms were not very fully defined, however, and
certain minor conclusions and testings were omitted. These
will now be presented in Part II.

The most important concern is that of the validity of the
indexes chosen to represent the factors in the election. These
will be taken up in order.

The influence of the foreign-born voters. This influence is
generally conceived as that of the naturalized foreign-born
citizens who voted in the election. With some observers it
may mean votes of the children of immigrants. With still

others it may mean that rather large section of recent immigration that has come from southwestern Europe. Perhaps
the most general idea is that of the recent immigrants who
are contrasted with the old American stock. To represent
this somewhat variously conceived concept we have used the
percentages of the adult population that were foreign-born
in 1920. The percentages have, it is thought, changed little
since 1920. Probably the correlation between the adult foreign-
born and the foreign-born voters is quite high. Also usually
in those counties where there is also a large percentage of
the children of foreign-born. The foreign-born are naturally
a heterogeneous group coming from various countries, linquis-
tic and racial stocks; but the current concept seems to take
them collectively. It has been argued that the foreign-born
in the large cities and the foreign-born in the smaller places
are two different types of individuals and do not belong to
the same series. Hence, a correlation with the percentage
of foreign-born in counties mixes two different things and
does not adequately test the support of the urban foreign-born
which is the group that is supposed to have supported Smith.
In many small industrial towns around factories or coal fields,
the foreign-born may not be greatly different from those
in the cities, except that in cities the foreign-born voters may
be more highly organized and more readily mobilized politically. In New York City, a city of many immigrants and
Smith's home city, the influence of the foreign-born was
greater, (the correlation based on aldermanic districts was
+.59), than in these counties throughout these different states
(the correlation being +.33). There is probably some difference between the measure of foreign-born influence within
the large cities and throughout the country.

   The religious influence. The Roman Catholics are supposed
to have thrown their support more strongly to Smith and the
Protestants more strongly to Hoover. There are of course
other religious groups than these. Yet the percentage of the
population that is Catholic is probably very highly correlated
negatively with the percentage of the population that is Prot-

estant. It was not possible to get the numbers of Catholics who were adults. The index that was used was the total number of Catholics of all ages in 1926, expressed as a percentage of the total population, estimated by the usual exponential curve, for that year. Catholic families are supposed to have a larger number of children than Protestant families, but such an error might be balanced by the fact that the age distribution of immigrants (who are often strongly Catholic) show few children.

The influence of the prohibition issue. There are many attitudes on this issue from bone dry to dripping wet. In general, those with any wet indications whatsoever were supposed to be sympathetic with the Democratic candidate. The problem was to find data that would show this sentiment. The most reliable index to be found was the vote on some phase of the prohibition question in those few states that had voted in recent years (1926, 1927, or 1928) on this question. The questions usually submitted to the voter in these state referendums were regarding the enforcement or repeal of the Volstead act or the sale of light wines and beers. The states, therefore, voted on different measures. In any one state the counties could be ranked on the proper scale of prohibition sentiment or vice versa. But for our analysis it was necessary to have all the counties of these different states ranked in one series. It was possible to link these counties of the different states together by using the data of the Literary Digest poll of 1922, when *one* question was submitted to samples of voters in *all* the states. From these votes it was thus possible to say, for instance, that if the wet sentiment in Illinois was 1, then in New York it was 1.2 and in Ohio it was .9. By utilizing such ratios the counties which were in proper alignment one with another in a particular state could be brought into a common line for all the states by stepping up or stepping down the actual issue by ratios such as the foregoing. This was done. As an experiment this alignment of counties in a series as adjusted by the state ratios of the Digest poll was correlated with the series of county votes thrown together as they were without stepping up or down. The coefficient of correlation was found to be +.83. Another test showed why so high a correlation was probable. In Illinois, the people voted in 1922 and in 1926 on two different measures, one permitting 4 per cent beer and light wines for home consumption and the other a modification of the Volstead Act. The correlation by counties of these two votes on two different measures 4 years apart was +.89. It would seem, therefore, that the index adjusted by the ratios of the Digest poll was a satisfactory one for measuring the differentials in prohibition feeling among the various counties.

The influence of party regularity. There is a concept of party allegiance and stability. For instance, one finds certain individuals regularly voting Democratic or there are certain states and counties that regularly go Republican. It was desired to hold this factor constant, in measuring the various other influences on the election, for the counties studied. This concept does not mean the average Democratic vote, but rather the solid, stable group that does not fluctuate in general from one party to another as the issues change. Such has been the idea of the solid Democartic party in the south. The actual size of this more or less stable Democratic vote must be then smaller than the average Democratic vote. The vote for Cox was taken as the index of traditional party influence so conceived, largely because of the complications of the La Follette vote in 1924. The Cox vote is said to be somewhat unrepresentative because of the defection of the foreign-born groups. This would render the Cox vote an unsatisfactory index of the average Democratic vote, but would give it greater validity as an index of regularity. Cox received a slightly larger percentage of the total vote (34) than did Davis (29). The correlation between the Smith vote and the Davis vote in the counties studied was +.13 while the correlation between the Smith vote and the Cox vote was +.12. The Wilson votes were rather far away and complicated by war influences. (The correlation between the Smith vote and the average of the Democratic votes of 1912, 1916, and 1920 was +.30.) The Cox

vote, it is thought, is therefore a reasonably good index of
this concept of party influence.

The urban influence. The Democratic candidate grew up
on the sidewalks of New York City and the cities are supposed to have voted for him. The index of the urban influence
was taken as the percentage of the population in a county
living in urban communities as defined by the U. S. Bureau
of Census namely, in places of 2500 inhabitants and over.
The dividing line at this point may set off the rural influences
better than the urban. For it is questionable whether what is
called urban influence begins to show itself in places as small
as 2500 inhabitants. A dweller in a very large city might argue that the urban influence he has in mind is not found in
cities of less than 100,000 inhabitants or perhaps not in cities
of less than 500,000 or 1,000,000 inhabitants. On the other
hand a dirt farmer living in the open country might notice
urban influences in towns of quite modest size. For the validity
of our index of urbanism, it is quite probable that the counties
which have the largest cities are also the ones which have the
largest percentage of the population living in places of over
2500. Certainly the converse is true, that the counties having
the largest percentages of population living in places of
less than 2500 inhabitants have the largest per cent of farmers.

In order to test this point further, the counties were classi-
fied as follows, those having cities under 10,000, those having
cities from 10,000 to 50,000, those with cities of over 100,000.
Each of these classes was then broken up into four classes
showing very low, low, high, and very high percentages of
votes cast for Smith. The coefficient of contingency was .28
which is not very different from the coefficient of correlation,
$+.16$, between the Smith vote for these same counties and the
percentage of urban dwellers as measured by the percentages
of the population living in places over 2500. The similarity
in the magnitude of these two coefficients gives confidence
in the index of urbanism used. The drift of the larger cities
toward Smith was not marked, as shown by our sample.